The Lite

Is Literatu

The Literary Agenda

Is Literature Healthy?

JOSIE BILLINGTON

OXFORD
UNIVERSITY PRESS

OXFORD
UNIVERSITY PRESS

Great Clarendon Street, Oxford, OX2 6DP,
United Kingdom

Oxford University Press is a department of the University of Oxford.
It furthers the University's objective of excellence in research, scholarship,
and education by publishing worldwide. Oxford is a registered trade mark of
Oxford University Press in the UK and in certain other countries

First Edition published in 2016

Impression: 1

Published in the United States of America by Oxford University Press
198 Madison Avenue, New York, NY 10016, United States of America

British Library Cataloguing in Publication Data
Data available

Library of Congress Control Number: 2016934844

ISBN 978-0-19-872469-8

Printed in Great Britain by
Clays Ltd, St Ives plc

for John and Sylvia

Series Introduction

The Crisis in, the Threat to, the Plight of the Humanities: enter these phrases in Google's search engine and there are 23 million results, in a great fifty-year-long cry of distress, outrage, fear, and melancholy. Grant, even, that every single anxiety and complaint in that catalogue of woe is fully justified—the lack of public support for the arts, the cutbacks in government funding for the humanities, the imminent transformation of a literary and verbal culture by visual/virtual/digital media, the decline of reading...And still, though it were all true, and just because it might be, there would remain the problem of the response itself. Too often there's recourse to the shrill moan of offended piety or a defeatist withdrawal into professionalism.

The Literary Agenda is a series of short polemical monographs that believes there is a great deal that needs to be said about the state of literary education inside schools and universities and more fundamentally about the importance of literature and of reading in the wider world. The category of 'the literary' has always been contentious. What *is* clear, however, is how increasingly it is dismissed or is unrecognised as a way of thinking or an arena for thought. It is sceptically challenged from within, for example, by the sometimes rival claims of cultural history, contextualized explanation, or media studies. It is shaken from without by even greater pressures: by economic exigency and the severe social attitudes that can follow from it; by technological change that may leave the traditional forms of serious human communication looking merely antiquated. For just these reasons this is the right time for renewal, to start reinvigorated work into the meaning and value of literary reading for the sake of the future.

It is certainly no time to retreat within institutional walls. For all the academic resistance to 'instrumentalism', to governmental measurements of public impact and practical utility, literature exists in and across society. The 'literary' is not pure or specialized or self-confined; it is not restricted to the practitioner in writing or the academic in studying. It exists in the whole range of the world which is its subject-matter: it consists in what non-writers actively receive from writings when, for example, they start to see the world more imaginatively as a result of reading novels and begin to think more carefully about human personality. It comes from literature making available much of human life that would not otherwise be existent to thought or recognizable as knowledge. If it is true that involvement in literature, so far from being a minority aesthetic, represents a significant contribution to the life of human thought, then that idea has to be argued at the public level without succumbing to a hollow rhetoric or bowing to a reductive world-view. Hence the effort of this series to take its place *between* literature and the world. The double-sided commitment to occupying that place and establishing its reality is the only 'agenda' here, without further prescription as to what should then be thought or done within it.

What is at stake is not simply some defensive or apologetic 'justification' in the abstract. The case as to why literature matters in the world not only has to be argued conceptually and strongly tested by thought, it should be given presence, performed and brought to life in the way that literature itself does. That is why this series includes the writers themselves, the novelists and poets, in order to try to close the gap between the thinking of the artists and the thinking of those who read and study them. It is why it also involves other kinds of thinkers—the philosopher, the theologian, the psychologist, the neuro-scientist— examining the role of literature within their own life's work and thought, and the effect of that work, in turn, upon literary thinking. This series admits and encourages personal voices in an unpredictable variety of individual approach and expression, speaking wherever possible across countries and disciplines and temperaments. It aims for something more than intellectual assent: rather the literary sense of what it is like to feel the thought, to embody an idea in a person, to bring it to being in a narrative or in aid of adventurous reflection. If the artists refer to their own works, if other thinkers return to ideas that have marked much of their working life, that is not their vanity nor a failure of originality. It is what the series has asked of them: to speak out of what they know and care about, in whatever language can best serve their most serious thinking, and without the necessity of trying to cover every issue or meet every objection in each volume.

Philip Davis

Contents

Introduction

This book is the result of a journey which began in 2008, when as an English Literature teacher at the University of Liverpool, I started to work with colleagues in medicine and psychology who were tackling mental ill health, depression in particular. 'Research' in my discipline had meant scholarly publications aimed exclusively at an audience of literary specialists. For my colleagues in medicine and psychology, Christopher Dowrick and Richard Bentall, and latterly Rhiannon Corcoran, research was part of an urgent struggle in relation to a worldwide epidemic. 350 million people suffer from depression globally according to World Health Organization figures. Over the next two decades, depression is set to overtake every other major health problem, including heart disease and cancer. What place could literature possibly have in this struggle? What could it *do*?

For Dowrick and Bentall, the battle seemed increasingly to be not against the illness, but against its diagnosis and treatment. 'Depression' is existentially broader and subtler as well as historically older and culturally deeper, than current medical understanding allows. Since the final decades of the last century, the influential dictionary of symptoms published by American psychiatry, the Diagnostic and Statistical Manual of Mental Disorders (DSM), has categorized depression as mild, moderate, or severe, according to the number of characteristic symptoms displayed (agitation, loss of energy, diminished pleasure or ability to concentrate) and how long they last. The subsequent emphasis on detection and treatment of depression in the US and UK in the 1990s coincided with the pharmaceutical marketing drive for Prozac.

But this rigid classification system not only divides the complex and heterogeneous experience of mental illness into distinct 'conditions';

it also divides mental illness from the normality of experience, or threatens to make common human sorrows—normality under severe strain—into an illness. A purely symptom-based diagnosis has led to the over-medicalization of suffering, 'treating' it with mass prescriptions of antidepressants, when such suffering might be an unavoidable, even necessary aspect of normal experience. 'Major depressive disorder has received more research attention than any other diagnosis in psychiatry but [the criteria] are so loose that, in everyday clinical practice, ordinary sadness can be easily confused with clinical depression.' What is called a 'depressive episode' and diagnosed as 'mental illness' may be 'better understood as normal intense sadness'.[1] This makes depression—which is common to us all—a crucial model for how the human condition can be 'medicalized'.

To give a current example. The recently revised DSM-V newly categorized the grief of bereavement as a depressive disorder if symptoms of 'major depressive disorder'—principally depressed mood and loss of interest or pleasure in nearly all activities—continue just two weeks after the loss of a loved one. Feelings of loss and emptiness following a bereavement are counted as 'the pain of grief' when 'accompanied by positive emotions and humour', but are to be diagnosed as a major depressive episode 'when, for most of the day, nearly every day, for at least two consecutive weeks, there is persistent depressed mood, pervasive unhappiness and misery, and the inability to anticipate happiness and pleasure'.[2] Almost contemporaneously with the appearance of DSM-V, in 2013, Julian Barnes published *Levels of Life*, a memoir of his wife, who died in 2008, in which he wrote: 'I already know that only the old words would do: death, grief, sorrow, sadness, heartbreak. Nothing modernly evasive or medicalizing. Grief is a human, not a medical, condition.'[3] It was not to be overcome in two weeks. 'Medical intrusion into private emotions,' says Dowrick, 'substitutes a superficial medical ritual for deep and time-honoured cultural ones.'

The medicalization and over-diagnosis of normal human nature, turning grief into a mental disorder and stigmatizing sadness with an illness label, are not merely the outcome of a pharmaceutical conspiracy. They are symptomatic of the focus in mental health on wanting to fix what is 'wrong' and thus, however worthy that ambition, of failing to bear to recognize that the typical causes of depression—loss, trauma, lack—are aspects of experience not susceptible to straightforward correction or cure.

My work with colleagues in medicine and psychology has helped me to see that depression is the flawed modern definition of the deep troubled life which, through the ages, it has been literature's task to express. I am not saying that literature is only about trouble; I am saying that its other virtues of celebration, of beauty, of immersed thought and feeling, are part of a vitality in existence. It is that vitality in sickness and in health that makes literature humanly expressive. But, as Dowrick insists in his own book, *Beyond Depression*, literature, in its deeper language of experience and emotion, radically challenges the conventional health-professional's view that sufferers diagnosed with depression are medically ill. It offers to those sufferers themselves a representation of sadness as a human norm—as though literature itself said implicitly 'Nothing human is alien to me'—without merely normalizing that experience in a reductive way.

This was a potent revelation; it was also a lifeline for me. The chief frustration and sadness of my own teaching life was that the discipline to which I belonged had, in part and at worst, lost a sense that literature might speak to humans' deepest needs. What mattered in English teaching from the final decades of the twentieth century was not the writer's personal expression of experience, but the student's ability to understand its historical context or the ideologies supposedly implicit within it. Any personal feeling a student might have for a poem or book was often deemed beside the point. The discipline seemed to me to be encouraging first-year students to believe that, armed with the smatterings of a sophisticated ideological or theoretical template, they had more to put upon the text than they had to learn or to be given by it. I have frequently come across graduates from degrees in English literature who say they have been put off reading in their subsequent lives by the way they had to study 'texts' at university. A common complaint and disappointment is that they spent more time reading and discussing critical 'books about books' than thinking about the novels and poems themselves. A current undergraduate at a prestigious university told me perplexedly that she didn't feel she'd had 'an idea of her own' since starting her degree; the message she had received was that personally 'original' thinking would not be rewarded with good marks.

No doubt, looking back, one reason that I began to find a more congenial home in the field, broadly speaking, of medical humanities was that this relatively new discipline had been founded upon frustrations and bafflement analogous to those I was experiencing.

The modern medical humanities movement, which began in North America in the 1960s, was principally a reaction against the highly focused biomedical and laboratory-based training which had characterized US medical education since the first decades of the twentieth century. It was a resistance to an over-rigid discipline like my own. The movement was specifically instigated by religious teachers. Chaplains posted to medical schools began conferring with physicians who were concerned to counter the emphasis on the role of the physician as primarily scientist, by giving humanities a place in medical education. In 1969, they founded The Society for Health and Human Values for 'persons committed to human values in medicine', now the American Society for Bioethics and Humanities (ASBH). In its broader secular development, medical humanities has come to include disciplines as diverse as literature, the visual and performing arts, the history of medicine, and bioethics. It claims a wide range of philosophical and political agendas, goals and purposes within the health curriculum, including the training of doctors in clinical empathy, critical thinking, ethical awareness, gender and race issues and cross-cultural medicine. Yet this diverse movement is held together principally by its insistence upon the presence of the first-person dimension in health as something more, and other, than a mere accompaniment to ostensibly objective medicalized measures.

Martyn Evans, one of the leaders in the medical humanities field in the UK, writes of the importance of recognizing the human body 'not only in medicine's conventional biological terms but also in sociological, philosophical, psychological and cultural terms':

> An understanding of this sort might enable us more concertedly to address the unhappiness and dissatisfactions of so many patients, which persist (increasingly so) despite unprecedented levels of health care spending, and which seem to disclose the 'somatisation' of problems experienced elsewhere in people's lives.[4]

By 'somatisation', Evans means two things: the treating of problems that might *originate* elsewhere—in social circumstances or psychological difficulties—as though they were in the *body*; and the possibility of bodily symptoms being an *expression* of trouble that is not essentially physical.

There is of course a history to the separation of the biological and social, psychological and philosophical, in understanding ill health. Early in the nineteenth-century, argues Edward S. Reed, the emerging discipline of psychology was 'a science of the soul'. The most important European psychologist was Erasmus Darwin, significantly at once 'a medical doctor, poet, and natural philosopher'.[5] When, from the 1850s, psychologists consistently avoided developing the philosophical implications of their work, narrowing their field to a laboratory-based science of the mind, what emerged was a discipline and a professionalism defined not so much by its discovery of a new field but by its abandonment of traditional allies: literature, philosophy, physiology. This creation of specialization was sensible and humane in intention; when what is urgently sought and desperately needed is a cure, then the creation of distinct disciplines with trained expertise in attaining definite physical outcomes feels like genuine progress.

And yet there was a cost in the separations involved. When George Eliot read Charles Darwin's *On the Origin of Species* on its first publication in 1859, she was an admirer: the book's 'elaborate exposition of the evidence in favour of the Development theory makes an epoch'. Yet, she added, 'to me the Development theory and all other explanations of processes by which things came to be, produce a feeble impression compared with the mystery that lies under the processes.'[6] For George Eliot, there was another level of understanding which was missing even from the fullest evolutionary explanation. It was this intuition that triggered the novelist in George Eliot. For that reason alone she is a crucial touchstone for this book. And yet she is also the writer who centres many of the issues I face in defending literature's role in the understanding of human processes. 'Mysteries' seems itself a 'feeble' word to set against Darwinian scientific rigour. You can imagine the scientist's retort: Mysteries! Isn't that what you literary types always say? So with literature: it can appear a merely soft and weak thing, with no relation, or contribution to make, to 'robust' knowledge, as if it were merely picking up what is omitted, or still holding on to what is left over, by other forms of understanding. In part, this has become literature's fate. T. E. Hulme famously called poetry from the Romantics onwards 'spilt religion',[7] as literature took over the function of religion in expressing and directing spiritual energies and needs. I cannot ignore the possibility that the most recent positioning of literature and reading within health might just be another version of a residual spillage. Even so, in what follows I shall seek to test the value of literature's language, in all its vulnerability, wherever it finds itself.

When I began to work more explicitly in the field of mental health, I knew relatively little of this history. What I did know was some part of Robert Burton's thinking in *The Anatomy of Melancholy*, which offers a more ancient, more 'holistic', understanding of what health is:

> What is sicknesse, but a dissolution or perturbation of the bodily league, which health combines: And who is not sick, or ill disposed, in whom doth not passion, anger, envie, discontent, feare & sorrow raigne? Who labours not of this disease?[8]

In the light of man's illnesses and afflictions, which Burton catalogues exhaustively, health is not an a priori state nor perhaps even a state that we have a right to expect. For sickness with health always, and quite normally, '*combines*', says Burton. 'Who is not sick?'

What I did know was how seemingly split up were the practices of the present. Not only was illness quarantined as a thing distinct from, and opposite to, health in most conventional specializations, but the medical discipline itself was separate from disciplines to which in earlier ages it had been more nearly allied. I was forcibly struck by this when, as part of my journey into the field of medical humanities, I moved out of a Department of English into an Institute of Psychology, Health and Society. This involved crossing physically from the modern side of campus into the grand origins of the university—the red-brick edifices which, at the end of the nineteenth century, had been incorporated into the newly established Liverpool Medical School, first founded earlier in the century to train doctors to cope with the city's cholera epidemics and other diseases besetting the urban poor. The building I now occupied was dedicated to training public health specialists and clinical psychologists, continuing a venerable and admirable tradition. It was no abstract question to ask: how does literature belong here? The language I loved would never appear in clinical health questionnaires. Yet it was here, as part of the practical effort to fulfil a pressing mental health agenda, that the deep content of literature now seemed to have its best chance of finding a meaningful place once again in the wider world. Still, I had reservations as to whether literature was merely healthy—either cheerily uplifting or a good place to go for the solution of problems.

The key concern for this present book is not knowing where to place reading in the modern world. It is a difficulty deeply connected to an inability to define or find a place for essential stuff—the good and the bad. The dominance of the diagnosis of depression on the one hand, and of the language and aspiration of 'health' or 'wellbeing' on the other, has coincided with the loss of frameworks and vital language for human purposes. It is as if 'mental health' tries to fill the vacuum left by both religion and poetry.

So perhaps that sense of the ill-fittingness of things—of the very things that seem really to belong together in the broad field of 'human understanding', like literature and psychology, for example— cannot be helped, given the dominant modes of modern thinking. We do not really know what constituted psychology before the nineteenth century, says Edward S. Reed, precisely because the study of 'the nature of vital and mental forces . . . did not fit straightforwardly into any single discipline'. Reed cites George Henry Lewes, founder of the psychology journal *Mind* and life-partner of George Eliot, as the last nineteenth-century thinker to embody this original 'interdisciplinarity' of the human sciences. An amateur experimentalist, political and literary journalist, and prolific biographer, Lewes's magisterial *Problems of Life and Mind* combines micro-physiology with Spinozist ethics to offer an integrative comprehension of body and mind as parallel aspects of one another (Reed, pp. x, 145–6). It is a form of thinking which has largely been lost in succeeding centuries.

In many ways, then, it is as if medical humanities as a field of pedagogy and research is seeking to put back together elements which were seamlessly whole in an older world, where any merely medical explanation of pain or unhappiness was demonstrably insufficient. It has sought to counter the false separations—body/mind, healthy/ ill—which followed from specialization. Now an established presence in medical education in over half of US and Canadian universities, and strongly influencing similar developments in UK higher education, medical humanities has, from the first, harnessed the resources of literature to its mission.

In her survey of four decades of medical humanities as a 'flourish-ing interdisciplinary field', Johanna Shapiro cites diverse instances of literature's power to enrich the medical curriculum. Reading liter-ature can help medical trainees to gain insight and sensitivity in areas that are 'difficult to fully apprehend from purely didactic instruction: the patient's experience of illness; difficult patient–physician interactions; breaking bad news'. Fiction can 'engender reflection in learners by incorporating radically different perspectives from those normally represented in medicine for apprehending and interpreting the world'. Poetry is valued because 'it does not rely entirely on ordinary logic, the preferred method of thinking in which medical students are trained...Poetry addresses things that cannot be said directly, that perhaps are only sensed intuitively rather than known through ordi-nary thinking.'[9]

Here is a glimpse of one of the earliest experiments in putting literature into medicine as a humanizing force. In 1978, Anthony R. Moore, a surgeon and medical teacher practising in Melbourne, wrote of his dissatisfaction with medical education for giving exclusive priority to producing qualified scientific experts. 'Think how great is the writing, time and money spent on medicine as a science. Then go into the wards and clinics and see the *human* we are asked to cope with. Our product is pure line but it lacks hybrid vigour.' 'Pure line' is a genetic term for species of animals and plants which retain consistent characteristics over successive generations as a result of inbreeding.

This is from the introduction to Moore's published account of his efforts to leaven clinical studies with something more informally human by delivering a short literature course for first-year medical students. The course was structured around extracts from classic literary works and Moore's book consists of transcripts of the audio-recorded sessions.

Here, in a representative example, the class are reading an extract from Theodore Dreiser's short story 'The Lost Phoebe'. It introduces Old Henry Reifsneider and his wife, Phoebe—a simple and 'loving couple', for whom, beyond the daily round of simple chores, 'there are no immediate significant things':

> Old Henry, who knew his wife would never leave him in any
> circumstances, used to speculate at times as to what he would do

if she were to die. That was the one leaving that he really feared. As he climbed on the chair at night to wind the old, long-pendulumed, double-weighted clock, or went finally to the front and back door to see that they were safely shut in, it was a comfort to know that Phoebe was there, properly ensconced on her side of the bed, and that if he stirred restlessly in the night, she would be there to ask what he wanted.

The group first commented on the extent of the husband's 'dependency' on his wife, how the couple 'live in their own world – all they've got is themselves'. One student felt there was an element of selfishness ('he wants feed for his security'). This response was still at the surface of what is happening—the usual language for personal relationships. But then a student called Nicholas said:

It's not just a matter of functional dependence. I would feel the same – that if you lose someone on whom you depend, that is a terrible thing. It feels almost as though you have lost half of yourself.

Nicholas noticed how the author describes 'common events'.

I could imagine the passage re-phrased with an emotionally descriptive approach, using words like 'love' and 'fear'. But instead of doing that he's made it very practical and real. These everyday events are carried over into what is happening emotionally.

Moore's book is full of these small instances of tonal or emotional 'correction', thinking on the margins of definite concept. It is *literary* thinking. Nicholas is taking his cue from what he recognizes in the writing: in place of straightforward or facile naming of feelings—'love', 'fear'—the story's language seems to *find* emotion embedded in 'the real'. Both reader and writer begin not with solid nouns and prior knowing, but with something more implicit and subtle—the 'carry over', as Nicholas calls it, between the literature and the life.

This is what Anthony Moore seems to have been looking for most of all. The unprogrammatic exercise of such thinking would help these trainee doctors believe in 'an area of conviction which lay outside the domain of scientific proof or test'. It was an area that would be required in response to the individual pain and suffering encountered in clinic or ward. Moore called his book *The Missing Medical Text*.[10] The careful and personal primary reading of literature which was being sometimes jettisoned by English studies, was the very thing felt to be missing in medicine—an essential part of the doctor's equipment. For me, this recognition offered the renewed sense of a need for my subject and promised a renaissance.

Yet, while the teaching of medical and psychology students did indeed offer one way out of a pedagogical dead end, it gave me first-hand understanding of why moving literature into health is both good and bad. Good, because it keeps the practice of literary reading alive, helpful in the wider world. I am very glad that literature is put to the valuable service of producing good doctors and clinicians. But it's not enough. Books exist to do more. I will argue that there is a danger, in current medical humanities practice, of the ancient partners of medicine and the humanities being put back together in a second-order, quasi-functional way, which cannot recover their essential primary connectedness—a 'misfitting' which is itself symptomatic of a loss of whole purposes.

For the chief contention of this book is not just that literature is too often what is missing from medical syllabuses and from theoretical approaches to the arts. It is missing most worryingly from *life*, from our normal ways of thinking. Just as my concern is not solely with depression nor is it simply with medicine. It's literature's *usefulness*—a place or space for that—that I'm really looking for.

My second contention is that literature is under-used and that its value and purpose is neglected but that this need not be the case. Much of what follows is based on my witnessing of and research into what is happening when people read novels, stories and poems together. The examples I give of real readers doing real reading—often people who are troubled, hurt or suffering—demonstrate how the widespread absence of reading from people's experience is neither necessary nor irrevocable.

Indeed, by far the best and most vital model for combining reading and health or crossing literature and medicine is *within* the individual reader—the person suffering depression reading a nineteenth-century sonnet, the chronic pain sufferer reading Dickens. This is hybrid vigour. For poetry and fiction do not have a health agenda; neither knows anything of cases or cures. For that reason, books can help to find something in the person that is not merely 'ill', or something in the illness that is not simply 'bad'. So-called 'negative' experience, as we shall see, can begin to be used as part of a continuum of existence, not just suffered.

At the same time, if illness is the extreme point on the spectrum of what is normal in coping with existence, then what we see in those cases where literature is useful to those who are suffering badly, is really only a more dramatic form of what literature can potentially offer to everybody, all of the time. As the ensuing chapters will show, what I call the 'right place' for literature is really something that literature itself creates, wherever and whenever it is read, by putting people, its readers, in the right place for the awakening of feeling and the vital beginning of thinking—the right place, that is, for being more fully alive.

****

Most of the chapters that follow centre on particular literary texts. I give notice of these here, in case it is helpful to the reader to be aware of them in advance. In Chapter One, I consider the potential therapeutic value of literary reading in relation to the work of the twentieth-century psychoanalyst Wilfred Bion and three nineteenth-century fictions: George Eliot's *Middlemarch* together with Leo Tolstoy's *Anna Karenina* and the novella *The Death of Ivan Ilyich*.

In Chapter Two, my concern is with the aspect of medical humanities that shares most affinity with the study of literature and literary processes: the widespread contemporary practice of encouraging patients to tell their own stories, provide their own narratives, in diagnosis and treatment. I focus on the seminal work in this field, Michael Balint's *The Doctor, his Patient and the Illness*, alongside George Eliot's first endeavours in literary story, *Janet's Repentance*, and Elizabeth Barrett Browning's nineteenth-century confessional poem, *Sonnets from the Portuguese*.

Chapter Three focuses on short quoted extracts from a range of works and periods as it records particular instances in the reading experience of individual readers, deriving from my current practical research into reading and health. Finally, Chapter Four concerns the foundational text for medical humanities: John Berger's celebrated mix of meditation, memoir, story, and photograph, *A Fortunate Man*, offered here as a paradigm for connecting medicine to literature, and literature to life.

Notes

1. Christopher Dowrick and Allen Frances, 'Medicalizing unhappiness', *British Medical Journal*, 2013, 347:f7140 doi: 10.1136/bmj.f7140 (Published 9 December 2013).
2. American Psychiatric Association Diagnostic and Statistical Manual of Mental Disorders, fifth edition (DSM-V) (2013), pp. 133–4.
3. Julian Barnes, *Levels of Life* (London: Jonathan Cape, 2013), p. 71.
4. Martyn Evans, 'Medical Humanities: What's in a Name?', *Journal of Medical Humanities*, 2002, 28:1–2. doi:10.1136/mh.28.1.1.
5. Edward S. Reed, *From Soul to Mind: The Emergence of Psychology* (New Haven: Yale University Press, 1997), pp. xi, 3.
6. Gordon S. Haight, *The George Eliot Letters*, 9 vols (New Haven and London, 1954–78), iii, pp. 214, 227.
7. T. E. Hulme, 'Romanticism and Classicism', in *Speculations: Essays on Humanism and the Philosophy of Art* (1924), ed. by Herbert Read (London: Routledge & Kegan Paul, 1960), pp. 113–40 (p. 118).
8. Robert Burton, *The Anatomy of Melancholy*, ed. Thomas C. Faulkner, Nicolas K. Kiessling and Rhonda L. Blair (Oxford: Clarendon Press, 1989), p. 25.
9. Johanna Shapiro, 'A Sampling of the Medical Humanities', 2006, *Journal for Learning through the Arts*, 2:1, 1–18, pp. 2, 6–7, 13.
10. Anthony R. Moore, *The Missing Medical Text* (Melbourne: Melbourne University Press, 1978), pp. 1–4, 40–4.

1

Healthy and Unhealthy Thoughts

I have argued that the 'depression' that is deemed a form of illness is often on the normal spectrum of human unhappiness. This chapter considers a 'disability' hidden behind depression which is possibly the secret cause of its felt want of a sense of meaning. I call the condition, following the principles of Wilfred Bion, 'not thinking', not being able to think.

Thoughts and Thinking: Bion's Theory

Born in India and educated in England, Wilfred Bion was a decorated tank commander in World War One, before reading history at Oxford and then medicine at University College, London. He joined the Tavistock Clinic as a psychoanalyst in 1932, counting Samuel Beckett among his clients. By the 1960s, he was Director of the London Clinic of Psychoanalysis and President of the British Psychoanalytic Society. Some of his most influential and pioneering work, however, took place during World War Two when he was based at the psychiatric military hospital, Northfield, treating servicemen suffering from 'war neurosis'—what we would now call 'post-traumatic stress'. Working experimentally in small groups with his patients, Bion encouraged close attention to what was happening for each individual, their moment by moment experience of the dynamics and tensions of the group itself. The idea was that by becoming aware of their feelings, the soldiers could begin to confront the complex emotions produced by their war trauma. The community of the rehabilitation wing needed to be in tune with such feeling before 'the full force of its energy could be released in self-cure'. What Bion encountered in the main, in fact, was hostility to change and a reluctance to face anxiety and fear. The real source of anxiety in these soldiers, Bion began to recognize, was the defences they had unconsciously erected against their distressing experiences, in order that they did not have to suffer their distress consciously. The patients expressed optimistic ideas or feelings of hope, diverting attention to some future event, away from Bion's insistence upon the immediate present: these rationalizations and displacements 'effected a compromise with feelings of guilt, hatred, destructiveness, despair'. But the real crux of the matter, Bion found, lay in the threat of any new idea or feeling to demand development and the inability to tolerate change:

> There is a hatred of having to learn by experience at all, and lack of faith in the worth of such a kind of learning. This is not simply a negative attitude; the process of development is really being compared with some other state... Something like arriving fully equipped as an adult fitted by instinct to know without training or development, without undergoing the pains of growth, exactly how to live and move and have his being.[1]

This crucial recognition of the existence of an instinctive 'hatred' of emotional and mental growth in those who most need it, was the beginning of Bion's 'theory of thinking'. It is often a difficult theory to grasp but there are certain key precepts.

> If a person cannot 'think' with his thoughts, that is to say that he has thoughts but lacks the apparatus of 'thinking' which enables him to use his thoughts, to think them as it were... then the personality is incapable of learning from experience.[2]

'Thoughts', for Bion, happen prior to thinking. 'Thinking' developed in response to the challenge presented by the existence of 'thoughts'— as a method or apparatus, that is, for dealing with them. Thought is not a product of thinking but a development forced on the psyche by the pressure of emotional experience and not the other way round. Bion called this capacity to think the 'alpha function'; thoughts are beta elements—the unmetabolized experiences that Bion's traumatized soldiers could not express—which are operated on, converted, digested, given a substance by thinking and thus made available for positive use, as 'alpha elements', in achieving fulfilment.[3] The more thoughts are thus worked on, transformed into realization, the more they are 'available for translation into action'. In the unhealthy psyche, thoughts are evaded, ejected, or stored as inert, undigested facts and symptoms:

> This failure is serious because in addition to the obvious penal-
> ties that follow from an inability to learn from experience there
> is a need for an awareness of an emotional experience, similar
> to the need for an awareness of concrete objects that is achieved
> through the sense impressions, because lack of such awareness
> implies a deprivation of truth and truth seems to be essential for
> psychic health.[4]

The focus of this chapter is on Bion's specific psychoanalytic concern with the damage done by *not* becoming conscious of feeling.

> The effect on the personality of deprivation [of truth] is analo-
> gous to the effect of physical starvation on the physique.... Failure
> to eat, drink or breathe properly has disastrous consequences
> for life itself. Failure to use the emotional experience produces a
> comparable disaster in the development of the personality.[5]

It is not life experience itself, or the emotion it induces, which presents the chief issue in healthy human development; rather, the critical matter is the inability to put the emotion to 'use' via realization *of* it, though on occasion the emotional content may itself be so terrible as to cause an inability to express it. Fear of dying—to give Bion's own example of the most common, mortal, universal, and terrible emotion—untranslated into a tolerable thought about itself, exists instead as a nameless dread. For Bion, as for Freud, psychological dis-ease, was in part the outcome of primitive psychic formations persisting inside advanced intelligences. Under the rule of the pleasure principle, said Freud, the governing purpose of psychical activity was to discharge painful material. Unconscious mental processes 'draw back from any event which might arouse unpleasure' and 'turn away from reality because it is found unbearable'. These are the 'older, primary processes, the residues of a phase of development in which they were the only kind of mental process'.[6] 'Freud assumes', says Adam Phillips in his introduction to Freud's writings, 'that the one thing the reader wants to do more than know, is not to know; that indeed, the very ways we go about knowing things is the form our greed for ignorance takes'.[7]

But it is as though, for Bion, ignorance is not so much greedily willed as it is radically our suffering condition, so multiple are the obstacles to adequate, healthy thinking. In the first place, the truth that is the object of our thinking—the thing in itself, the really real, which Bion designates 'O'[8]—proves intolerably frustrating precisely because it cannot be truly known except by experience or discovery:

> Reality is not something which lends itself to being known. It is impossible to know reality for the same reason that makes it impossible to sing potatoes; they may be grown, or pulled, or eaten, but not sung. Reality has to be 'been': there should be a transitive verb 'to be' expressly for use with the term 'reality'.[9]

The really real is lived, experienced in absorption, it is not abstractly comprehended. What is more, the thinking tools that are at our disposal—our mental or verbal 'containers' for the experience of reality—are liable, in the very effort at containment, to falsify or mis-represent through over-definition or inadequate frameworks:

> The words I write are supposed to 'contain' a meaning. The verbal expression can be so formalized, so rigid, so filled with already existing ideas that the idea I want to express can have all the life squeezed out of it. On the other hand, the meaning I want to express may have such force and vitality, relative to the verbal formulation in which I would strive to contain it, that it destroys the verbal container. . . . The con-tainer can squeeze everything 'out of' the contained; or the 'pressure' may be exerted by the contained so that the con-tainer disintegrates. An illustration would be the word used as a metaphor until the background is lost and the word loses its meaning.[10]

In particular, this problem might apply, paradoxically, to therapeutic containers. Think, for example, of the formulation, 'I am an alco-holic', which is universally encouraged in therapy groups for addic-tion. The sentence might be essential not only as a first step in acceptance of the problem, but in externally 'holding' its potentially explosive inner pain. Equally, there is the danger that this brave admis-sion becomes, through public repetition or familiarity, an automatic

language and default attitude which blots out the suffering reality that
it contains:

> Learning *depends* on the capacity to remain integrated and yet
> lose rigidity. This is the foundation of the state of mind of the
> individual who can retain his knowledge and past experience
> and yet be prepared to reconstrue past experiences in a man-
> ner that enables him to be receptive to a new idea. [my
> emphasis][11]

At the crux of Bion's thesis, as we shall see in the course of this chapter, is the contention that certain modes of human thinking are precisely ways of *not* thinking. 'Positive thinking' is arguably the most
insidious form, I shall suggest, since it poses as the healthy option by
deliberately excluding what Bion calls the 'negative realization'.[12]

Quite simply, as a species, humans are not readily equipped to
think. Thinking, Bion says, 'is embryonic even in the adult and has yet
to be developed fully by the race'. Indeed, the discovery of psychoanalysis, he claims, is itself a symptom of the fact that thinking and the
tasks of self-knowledge have been forced upon a mentality ill-suited
and underdeveloped for the purpose:

> An apparatus existed and had to undergo, still has to undergo,
> adaptation to the new tasks involved in meeting the demands of
> reality by developing a capacity for thought. The apparatus that
> has to undergo this adaptation is that which dealt originally
> with sense impressions relating to the alimentary canal.[13]

The 'older, primary processes' do not simply survive in humans; they
are, fundamentally, all we have. Thus in evolutionary and individual
terms, alpha function—the capacity to think thoughts, learn from
experience and thus ensure psychic wellbeing—itself needs help.

It is the contention of this book that literature has a role and power
analogous to that of psychoanalysis in amending and aiding depriva-
tions in human thought function. Moreover, as this chapter will show,
literature's power—to avert or alleviate the disastrous human consequences of not thinking one's thoughts—derives, in part, from its
capacity to recognize and demonstrate that disaster. Bion's work is this
book's first key to unlock how literature might aid the difficult task of
real thinking.

The literary examples which follow in this chapter are exclusively from nineteenth-century realist texts. The reason for this choice is not that other forms and periods of literature—Shakespearean drama, Romantic poetry—would not have served equally well to demonstrate what is essential and vital in problems of thinking and mind. The choice rests on the fact that quintessential literary realism (as exemplified principally in this chapter by Leo Tolstoy, and also by George Eliot) represents human difficulties with all the common messiness and complicating determinants, and often the surface invisibility and intractability, which they possess in ordinary reality. The problem of thinking is witnessed in its natural habitat, as it were.

Proto-Thoughts

For a literary representation of the central problem—the difficulty of adequately thinking one's own experience from within its struggling midst—I take Dorothea Brooke, in George Eliot's *Middlemarch*, here on honeymoon after her dreadfully innocent mistake of marrying the much older cleric scholar, Mr Casaubon. I choose this example in part because it is explicitly offered by George Eliot as an example of normal unhappiness—nothing 'very exceptional'. 'Many souls in their young nudity are tumbled out among incongruities and left to "find their feet" among them...Some discouragement, some faintness of heart...is not unusual':

> However, Dorothea was crying, and if she had been required to state the cause, she could only have done so in some such general words as I have used: to have been driven to be more particular would have been like trying to give a history of the lights and shadows; for that new real future which was replacing the imaginary drew its material from the endless minutiae by which her view of Mr Casaubon and her wifely relation, now that she was married to him, was gradually changing with the secret motion of a watch-hand from what it had been in her maiden dream. It was too early yet for her fully to recognise or at least admit the change, still more for her to have readjusted that devotedness which was so necessary a part of her mental life that she was almost sure sooner or later to recover it. Permanent

rebellion, the disorder of a life without some loving reverent resolve, was not possible to her; but she was now in an interval when the very force of her nature heightened its confusion.[14]

Dorothea cannot identify the cause of her unhappiness in part because that cause is a hidden and continuing process, not the clear thing it might seem to be, 'now that she was married to [Mr Casaubon]'. As George Eliot pityingly looks on, all too conscious of being able to articulate what Dorothea cannot, the shift from girlish ideal to married reality is happening so far inside the 'endless minutiae' of mundane ordinariness, that the very fact of change is not 'yet' clear for Dorothea, precisely because it is happening. This is not, for Dorothea, an 'interval' in which progress is being made from one state to another. The loss of a normative framework is deeply connected to the inexpressibility of the experience. Dorothea's crying—'the primary and natural expression of suffering and mental distress'[15]— seems deeply primitive here for being a symptom of her radical inarticulacy.

The existence of something incontrovertibly wrong but not identifiably *there* ('to have been driven to be more particular would have been like trying to give a history of the lights and shadows') is where, says Bion, proto-thoughts begin. These inchoate, half-commenced thoughts originate in the sensation of need, lack or that unnameable crisis when nothing outside clearly signals what it is that is wrong. If there is 'no thing', then 'no thing' is 'a thought'.[16]

At such moments as this from *Middlemarch*, literary language shows human thought coming into being, by articulately inhabiting those painfully suffered gaps which paradoxically generate thought's substance. In analogous imitation of her scientist character, Lydgate, George Eliot's humanely imaginative analysis 'pierces the obscurity of those minute processes which prepare human misery and joy...the first lurking-places...which determine the growth of happy or unhappy consciousness' (Chapter Sixteen). George Eliot's language in lieu of Dorothea's crying, occupies the barely experienceable 'intervals' where things happen, where big things originate themselves, *secretly*—before they can emerge in explicit formulation. 'It was *too early yet* for her *fully* to *recognise* or at least *admit* the change'. The recognition of unhappiness and loss must be psychologically admissible before healthily authentic realignment of thinking to present circumstances is possible at all. But they are still what is happening to her. For the really real matter—Bion's 0—is deep inside realism's predicament not something available outside and above it.

'An emotion which is a passion is a confused idea,' says Spinoza in George Eliot's translation of his *Ethics* where Spinoza is, so to speak, George Eliot's Bion, the thinker who knows what is and is not true thinking, in the midst of psychological difficulty:

> Our mind is necessarily active so far as it has adequate ideas... necessarily passive so far as it has inadequate ideas.... The better we know or understand an emotion... the more it is in our power, and the less the mind suffers from it.... That mind suffers most... which chiefly consists of inadequate ideas, so that it is characterised more by what it suffers than by what it does.[17]

George Eliot says of Dorothea's current inadequacy that she lived on with 'no distinctly shapen grievance that she could state even to herself... and in the midst of her confused thought and passion, the mental act that was struggling forth into clearness was a self-accusing cry that her feeling of desolation was the fault of her own spiritual poverty' (Chapter Twenty). 'The mental act... struggling forth into clearness' demonstrates why we need George Eliot's language to release the meaning of Dorothea's predicament on her behalf—to articulate thoughts which strictly belong to Dorothea but which, authentically immersed in that predicament, she cannot yet formally think for herself. This is what George Eliot's literary language might do, I shall be arguing in Chapter Two, on behalf of the species.

Yet there is a further strong sign here of how literary language might operate as an intermediary in human unhappiness, by offering alternative models of what 'depression' constitutes on the spectrum of illness to wellbeing. Dorothea's life energy is not lost; she endures, though paradoxically 'the very force of her nature heightened its confusion.' It is that same power, the very *best* of Dorothea that is making her situation worse. The suggestion here is that what we call depression might be the very opposite of loss of vital powers, or a deficiency in engaging with experience.

Pseudo-Thoughts

Let me put immediately next to Dorothea's struggle to mentalize her 'new real future', this rich Tolstoyan counter-model—Anna Karenina's beginning of a new life with Vronsky.

Having left Karenin and taken up with her lover abroad, Anna finds that she is 'unpardonably' happy:

> The memory of her husband's unhappiness did not poison her happiness. This memory was, on the one hand, too terrible to think of. On the other hand, her husband's unhappiness had given her too great a happiness to be repentant. The memory of all that had happened to her after her illness: the reconciliation with her husband, the break-up, the news of Vronsky's wound, his appearance, the preparation for the divorce, the departure from her husband's house, the leavetaking from her son – all this seemed to her a feverish dream from which she awakened alone with Vronsky abroad. (Book Five, Chapter Eight)[18]

I have chosen Richard Pevear's and Larissa Volokhonsky's modern translation for its attention to precise literal accuracy. (I have also consulted the original Russian text as a check and guide at all times, in what follows.) Aylmer Maude's translation—usually, for this writer, the translation of choice owing to Maude's personal knowledge of Tolstoy—reads in this instance: 'On the one hand this memory was too terrible to dwell upon, and on the other hand her husband's misfortune had meant for her too great a joy for repentance to be possible'. But it is crucial to a sense of the shape of Anna's thinking here that the 'on the one hand...on the other hand' clauses are two distinct sentences, as they are in the original Russian. Neither of them is for her to be thought if she is to be happy. Only Tolstoy sees how they both work together, from separate angles. It is precisely because what is 'terrible' in her husband's situation and what is 'great' in her own are all too incompatibly linked that their connection is literally unthinkable for Anna. Separating, one from another, the painfully contradictory elements that constitute her own experience of marriage, is just what Dorothea, of course, emphatically could not and would not do. In Anna, by contrast, Tolstoy presents a mind at some

level almost deliberately not making the painful connections. Bion
could offer a diagnosis:

> There are people whose contact with reality presents most diffi-
> culty when that reality is their own mental state.... People exist
> who are so intolerant of pain or frustration (or in whom pain
> and frustration is so intolerable) that they feel the pain but will
> not suffer it and so cannot be said to discover it.[19]

These 'un-thought' psychic materials—proto-thoughts so painful that
the psyche cannot tolerate the thinking of them—are what Bion
defines as 'beta elements', 'bad' objects not to be tolerated. The problem requires thought for a solution, says Bion, since thought, through
transformation of the primitive preverbal material, 'liberates the
intuition'.[20]

There is probably no better literary example or representation of
the mind as a form of primitive 'evacuatory musculature',[21] avoiding
and denying its thoughts, than the final movement of Tolstoy's
paragraph:

> The memory of the evil done to her husband aroused in her a
> feeling akin to revulsion and similar to that experienced by a
> drowning man who has torn away another man clinging to him.
> That other was drowned. Of course, it was bad, but it was the
> only salvation, and it was better not to remember those dreadful
> details.

'That other was drowned' is a reflex expulsion of three painful
thoughts in one human object: 'the evil done to her husband', the
'revulsion' aroused by its memory, and the rejected husband himself.
Revulsion is not just a reaction to her husband. Her 'feeling'—the
Russian word is closer to visceral 'sensation'—is an instinctive defence
against feeling at first hand the self-revulsion of guilt. 'Akin' is an
inspired translation of the Russian word 'like' when likeness is so
familial. The 'terrible unhappiness' of Karenin and her own 'great
happiness' point to the same reaction—not remembering, not thinking. Mind, instead, looks to life as a distraction from itself, reactively
putting Vronsky where Karenin used to be. *People* in place of *thoughts* is
Anna's rule, disastrously. 'Whatever substitute a person finds for
thought is *not* to be classified as thought,' says Bion [my emphasis].[22]

For substitutes can only displace, reproduce or repeat; they cannot lead transformatively to realization and reconstitution. 'спасенье', translated here as 'salvation' (and thus with its original religious meaning, derived from 'Спас', the Saviour) is translated by Aylmer Maude more prosaically as 'escape'. The existence of both meanings in the Russian implies how 'getting away with it' at one level of self has deeply serious consequences at the level of deep being or 'soul'.

****

Question 7 on the most recent General Health Questionnaire (GHQ 12) asks respondents: 'Have you recently been able to enjoy your normal day-to-day activities?' Question 12 asks: 'Have you recently been feeling reasonably happy, all things considered?' In the more nuanced Becks Depression Inventory (BDI) respondents are asked to choose a statement across a spectrum of emotional intensity: from 'I do not feel sad' to 'I am so sad or unhappy that I can't stand it' (Question 1); 'I am not particularly discouraged about the future' to 'I feel that the future is hopeless and that things cannot improve' (Question 2). It is not difficult to recognize that, judging by their likely scores on a GHQ 12 or the BDI, Anna would appear to a health practitioner in better psychic shape than Dorothea. What is much harder to decide is which of the following likely scenarios is the more worrying: that, on the one hand, Dorothea, on the basis of this diagnosis, would probably be prescribed medication; or, on the other, that the psychological damage in Anna would likely go unnoticed, not demonstrably in need even of psychosocial intervention.

This is a rather stark example of the limitations of contemporary discourse and diagnostic instruments around human trouble. It is the novelists, the philosophers and the psychoanalysts—and preferably some amalgam of all three—who make a better diagnosis. The nineteenth-century existentialist philosopher, Kierkegaard, would say of Anna's 'Of course, it was bad, but it was the only salvation', 'What [she] says is in a sense true, only not in the way she understands it.' So says Kierkegaard of the person living 'merely in the category of the immediate . . . knowing himself only in externals':

> He is turned around and what he says must be understood backwards; he stands there pointing to something that is not

despair, explaining that he is in despair, and yet, sure enough, the despair is going on behind him unawares. It is as though someone were standing with his back turned to the Town Hall and Court House, pointed straight ahead and said: 'There are the Town Hall and Court House.' The man is right, they are there – when he turns around.[23]

Anna's so-called salvation is a term that needs to be turned around. She is Tolstoy's version of the Kierkegaardian human disaster wherein a person becomes a self only through evasion of what she really is. For Bion, similarly, perpetual sickness is the psychic result of a person's not bearing to turn around and face his or her sickness in the here and now. What exists indeterminably, as a thing unacknowledged, must be 'there' interminably.

These are severe truths which yet need a place and language in the world. Literature's own special power is its capacity to find these great human problems still inside the smallest human instances; I want to show that the novelist here is in fact implicitly that amalgam of philosopher and psychoanalyst if we would recognize it.

****

Anna, for all the success of her evasive strategies, is not as ignorant of her problems as she would like to be. In the first moment of her new life, Anna half-thinks of all the bad things that went before: 'All this seemed to her a feverish dream from which she awakened *alone with Vronsky* abroad.' In this unexpected formulation ('together with' would be the natural collocation), she is more terribly isolated than Dorothea. This is how Anna goes on in the very next paragraph. Anna has left her son Serezha with her husband, taking her baby daughter, by Vronsky, abroad with them:

> One soothing reflection about her behaviour had occurred to her then, in the first moment of the break-up, and now when she remembered all that had happened, she remembered that one reflection. 'It was inevitable that I would be this man's unhappiness,' she thought, 'but I don't want to take advantage of that unhappiness; I, too, suffer and will suffer: I am deprived of all that I once valued most – my good name and my son. I did a bad thing, and therefore I do not want happiness, I do not

want a divorce, and will suffer from my disgrace and from my
separation from my son.' But however sincerely Anna wanted to
suffer, she did not suffer. There was no disgrace. With the tact
they both had so much of, they managed, by avoiding Russian
ladies abroad, never to put themselves in a false position and
everywhere met people who pretended that they fully understood their mutual position far better than they themselves did.
Even the separation from her son, whom she loved, did not torment her at first. The little girl, his child, was so sweet, and
Anna had become so attached to her, once this little girl was all
she had left, that she rarely remembered her son.

The preceding paragraph ended with the mental decision not to
remember the 'dreadful details'. Here, as if the gap between the para-
graphs were a physical representation of the not-thought or not-recalled
inside Anna's mind, the new paragraph begins with the same willed
pseudo-thinking by which Anna evaded suffering the break-up at the
time of its happening! The deep cost of substituting people for her own
unbearable thoughts is felt most keenly in the personal pronouns of this
passage. The repeated grammar of possession which seems to denote a
simple matter of biological fact in these recurring instances—'The
leavetaking from *her* son. . . . The separation from *my* son. . . . The separation from *her* son, whom she loved'—becomes a devastating sign of
'break-up' and incoherence in her current life and partnership in this
context: 'The little girl, *his* child, was so sweet, and Anna had become so
attached to her, once this little girl was all she had left, that she rarely
remembered *her* son.' The tiny grammatical shock gives retrospective
power to the twin movements of the penultimate sentence: 'Even the
separation from *her son, whom she loved*, did not torment her *at first*.' 'She
loved' is not narrative's simple past tense but the continuous present of
ill-placed maternity. In Dorothea's sequence—'It was too early yet for
her fully to recognise or admit the change'—the future was summoned
by that tiny temporal word 'yet', offering the certainty of adjustment at
some point ahead, even because of Dorothea's honest, blind, bewil-
dered forgoing of all hope of such adaptation to her situation. This was
alpha function doing its work as secretly as time's watch hand; the contrast is with 'at first' in Anna's sequence, left hanging at the end of the
line. It is a nemesis in waiting which is registered biologically in this
devastatingly simple syntax of mother–child identity.

D. H. Lawrence, thinking of his own elopement with a married woman who left behind her children, said 'the judgment of man' killed Anna, not 'the judgment of her own soul'.[24] But, in *Modern Tragedy*, Raymond Williams wrote: 'The social convention invoked against Anna is indeed shallow and hypocritical, but take a society in which there is no difficulty in divorce, in which an Anna would not be pointed at and avoided, and the human difficulty in substance remains. The child of the body is there in any society.'[25] It is an important reminder that primal realities which were once the public stuff of ancient tragedy are now private, hidden, psychic events—normalized as current divorce figures suggest. Not that I speak against divorce; but against what is forgotten when the word 'separation' is used too easily, in a way it could not be used in a more literary context. It is possible that a great deal of post-break-up depression is exacerbated by 'separation' in Western culture having become an unfortunately acceptable social and legal phenomenon, rather than being acknowledged as a deep psychic disturbance in need of help to realize itself. And that is a realization not unsympathetic to those who have to separate or cause separation.

Alpha Thoughts

What would human thinking at its honest best be like in relation to experience?

In *Anna Karenina*, it is Levin who provides the countermodel to Anna. Yet Levin is chosen as a template for 'healthy' thinking here not for the reason that he is 'better' at overcoming the strangeness of human thinking to human experience but because he more authentically embodies precisely that problem. For Levin is the man who constitutionally cannot live *without* thought, and yet hardly knows where thoughts belong in an incontrovertibly physical life.

More explicitly, strenuously and resistingly than Dorothea, and more in love than in sorrow, Levin, three months into his new life with Kitty, finds that married life is not a settled conclusion to his bachelor life but the opposite—a new and bewildering beginning:

> He was happy, but not at all in the way he had expected. At every step he found disenchantment with his old dream and a new, unexpected enchantment. He was happy, but, having

entered upon family life, he saw at every step that it was not
what he had imagined. At every step he felt like a man who,
after having admired a little boat going smoothly and happily
on a lake, then got into this boat. He saw that it was not enough
to sit straight without rocking; he also had to keep in mind, not
forgetting for a minute, where he was going, that there was
water underneath, and that he had to row, and his unaccustomed hands hurt. (Book Five, Chapter Fourteen)

The form of a loving marriage is not, as Levin had imagined, a ready-
made mode of existence. On the contrary, the form of his new life with
Kitty, must be made, he finds, as it goes along, in the necessary effort to
keep going in disconcerting ignorance of the course or direction which
beforehand had seemed so assured. It is only from inside that Levin can
know what being on board is really like. And inside the perplexing reality of his new situation he is too busy coping as best he can, ill-prepared
and inadequate, to be able stably, reliably, and reflectively to think
about it. 'It was easy only to look at, but doing it, while very joyful, was
also very difficult.' It's as if the difficult 'doing' *is* the thinking here. In
Levin's baffled, immersed syntax—'only . . . but . . . while . . . also', it is not
only his marriage which is 'shaping itself' (сложилась) but his mind
also, in the involuntary realignment of one with the other.

The image of Levin's predicament offers a wonderfully ordinary
and practical object lesson in Bion's account of the resistant relationship between 'container' and 'contained'. While the little boat 'holds'
Levin's ideal of loving union, the facts of married life—the 'fluidity'
of 0, the really real—'gird against' the rigid framework of definition,
and cannot be bound within existing formulations.[26] Yet at the same
time the reality does not utterly destroy the container, the prior ideal,
but revises and reintegrates it.

The process is unmistakably visible when, after the first matrimo-
nial quarrel with his wife, Levin 'understood [понял] clearly for the
first time what he had not understood [понимал] when he had led her
out of the church after the wedding'. In both instances above, as in the
two instances below, 'understood' derives from the same Russian verb,
[понимать]:

> He understood [понял] not only that she was close to him, but
> that he no longer knew where she ended and he began. He

understood [понял] it by the painful feeling of being split [раздвоения, literally 'division'—'раз'—'into two'—'двое'] which he experienced at that moment.[27]

'Understood', thus repeated registers, paradoxically, a kind of stunned disbelief. It is closer to resistant admission of what he does not wish to understand—'not only . . . but . . . no longer'—than achieved revelation of something he does recognize. Yet what Levin actually gets is only distinct from the cliché he expects in so far as it is now translated into the 'really real' version of itself. And the sign of its being really real is that the union is also unexpectedly experienced as a division of himself. That almost *comically* character proposes (i), and life disposes (ii)—in that order—is the life-system which the very shape of this prose doggedly insists upon; my notation here highlights it:

> [i] He was offended at first, but [ii] in that same instant he felt that he could not be offended by her, that she was him. In the first moment [i] he felt like a man who, having suddenly received a violent blow from behind, turns with vexation and a desire for revenge to find out who did it, and [ii] realizes that he has accidentally struck himself, that there is no one to be angry with and he must endure and ease the pain.

Significantly, 'understand' ['понял'] is not repeated in the sentence above but transposed to a more profoundly involuntary recognition—'убеждается', translated as 'realizes' and meaning 'persuaded' or 'certain of' at the level of earnest conviction or powerful belief. Realization happens at a deeper level *inside* Levin (and in the very middle of each sentence) when he finds himself the less able to get outside or ahead of the non-negotiable sequence of experience. Here my numbering seeks to show two distinct sorts of movement recurring:

> Natural feeling [i] demanded that he vindicate himself, prove to her that she was wrong; but [ii] to prove that she was wrong would mean to upset her still more and make the breach that had caused all the trouble still wider. [i] One habitual feeling urged him to shift the blame from himself to her; [ii] another, stronger one urged him quickly, as quickly as possible, to smooth

over the breach and keep it from growing bigger. [i] To remain under so unjust an accusation was tormenting, [ii] but to hurt her by vindicating himself was still worse. [i] Like a man suffering from pain while half-asleep, he wanted to tear off, to throw away the sore spot and, [ii] coming to his senses, found that the sore spot was himself.

While the (i) clauses stubbornly defend Levin's original, and still primary, sense of his own separate and absolute identity, the (ii) clauses swing back six times to invalidate those first impulses, saying to Levin '*This* is marriage—no longer being single.' It is vital that both remain in the same sentence. Real thinking—realization, understanding, alpha function—is created precisely out of the tension *between* the supposed or naïve idea (i), the modifying real (ii), and, within the latter, the really real version of the ideal (0), re-emergent within the texture of existence.

Only literature would insist that at such moments it is syntax itself that is the marker of a sort of health in truth. One of the most popular current models for healthy calibration of thought and feeling—for example, online mindfulness manuals—offer these bullet-point sentences for how to 'reduce vulnerability to...that state where we are ruled by our Emotion Mind, instead of our Wise Mind':

> To be at our best in dealing with our emotions, remember and
> **PLEASE MASTER:**
> Treat physical illness
> Balance eating
> Avoid mood-altering drugs
> Balance sleep
> Get Exercise
> Build mastery
> Increase positive emotions
> Find some ways to have fun.[28]

These rules are not useless or lacking in sense. But they could make no sense to a Levin who is struggling precisely with what are called here 'positive emotions': 'He was happy'! Levin has to find wisdom not in place of, or over and above, emotion but *inside* it, while he is being knocked *off*-balance 'at every step'. Levin cannot get to (ii) without first starting from (i).

What these literary texts offer, by contrast with modern self-help guides, is the unbalancing thought that in order to learn from experience, the evolutionary process may well have to be gone through again at every new life stage. For thoughts to emerge in the right way, at the right time—for real learning to happen—even the most evolutionarily developed human organism might have to begin again with the primary emotional material of experience, as from bottom-up. George Eliot and Tolstoy are literature's best witnesses of how there are no shortcuts in real thinking. They exemplify literary thinking's crucial capacity to 'detach itself from the *already-made* and attach itself to the *being-made*'. Thus, to do what philosophy needs to do, and often neglects to do, according to Henri Bergson:

> There is no durable system that is not, at least in some of its parts, vivified by intuition.... The philosopher is obliged to abandon intuition, once he has received from it the impetus, and to rely on himself to carry on the movement by pushing the concepts one after another. But he soon feels he has lost his foothold; he must come into touch with intuition again ... Fugitive and incomplete, it is, in each system, what is worth more than the system and survives it.[29]

'Thought without content is empty,' as Kant put it, 'intuition without concept is blind.'[30] This is the great idea that lies behind Bion's psychoanalytic theory of thinking. Neither intuition nor concept are sufficient on their own: each needs to 'come into touch' with the other in the right way at the right time, and repeatedly. This is no exact science, yet it involves the minutest precision. Perhaps only literature's richly amorphous 'system' can authentically capture these fine, fleeting instances.

For a final example. Dorothea's unhappiness is only properly known to *have been* a beginning in the light of this moment, several chapters later, now after the Casaubons' first marital quarrel:

> Today she had begun to see that she had been under a wild illusion in expecting a response to her feeling from Mr Casaubon, and she had felt the waking of a presentiment that there might be a sad consciousness in his life which made as great a need on his side as on her own ... It had been easier to her to imagine

how she would devote herself to Mr Casaubon, and become
wise and strong in his strength and wisdom, than to conceive
with that distinctness which is no longer reflection but feeling –
an idea wrought back to the directness of sense, like the solidity
of objects – that he had an equivalent centre of self, whence the
lights and shadows must always fall with a certain difference.
(Chapter Twenty-two)

Here is the adjustment promised by that tiny 'yet' in the earlier passage. It is a new beginning, a new growth ('She had begun to see'). It
is the kind of more profound self-help that Bion and Spinoza are looking for: the translation of raw inchoate emotion into a commensurate
thought which brings release and active life. George Eliot herself calls
it an 'epoch' in Dorothea's existence.

Yet the verbs that carry this creative power—'begun' and especially
'conceive'—belong as much to George Eliot as they do to her character. Language itself here, growing out of the writer's deep immersion
in this imagined particular life, is palpably 'emergent'—George Henry
Lewes's scientific term for the chemical phenomenon where proper-
ties do not simply mix (a 'resultant' effect) but produce something
entirely new.[31] Indeed, it almost has to be the writer and not the character here in whom intuition crystallizes into new recognition: it has
to be George Eliot, so to speak, who thinks Dorothea's half-thoughts
for her. For the realization of her own and Casaubon's shared 'equiv-
alence' of being is hard enough—the thought of living in the same
world with another who is a separate world unto himself. But it is also
testimony here that, together in marriage, sharing the same *life*, the
couple are mutually sundered. This is a terrible and lonely moment
even as it is a great one—the sort of profound and painful separation,
also 'not unusual', for which there are no statistics, nor usually any
external witness. But how could one ever be one's *own* witness to this
and simply carry on? How is this deeply inconsolable recognition even
possible as a thought, as a 'solid' idea, for the person to whom it
belongs? It is something barely thinkable except inside the book, yet
also barely avoidable at times in the world outside.

It is to this, then, that I now turn: literature's power to hold
thoughts which humans feel it would almost kill them to contain in
themselves.

Unthinkable Thoughts

At the age of forty-five, Ivan Ilyich is enjoying midlife success as a high
court judge with all the trappings of conventional middle-class life—an
up-market house, a 'contented' family, and acquaintance with 'the best
society'. His life, as he puts it, is 'easy, pleasant and decent'. When, after
a minor domestic fall, he begins to be troubled by a pain in his stomach,
he at first dismisses it as unimportant. Then, as the discomfort and his
irritability worsen, he consults doctor after doctor. The reading of medical books and accounts of illness and health become his 'main occupation'. Even while daily he loses strength, and becomes more estranged
from family and colleagues, Ivan Ilyich tries to manage his illness with
the efficiency that has hitherto served him so well in the law court:

> There was a little thing, a tiny little thing in the appendix. This
> could all be put right. [...] In his imagination the desired
> mending of the appendix was taking place. Absorption, ejec-
> tion, restoration of the correct functioning. 'Yes, that's all so,'
> he said to himself. 'One need only assist nature.' He remem-
> bered about his medicine, got up, took it, and lay on his back,
> waiting to feel the beneficial effect of the medicine and how it
> killed the pain. 'Just take it regularly and avoid harmful influ-
> ences; even now I feel a little better, a lot better.' He began to
> touch his side – it did not hurt. 'Yes, I don't feel it, truly, it's
> already much better.' (*The Death of Ivan Ilyich*, Chapter Five)[32]

Ivan Ilyich's official accounting of his illness places him entirely in
control of 'putting it right', exactly as if the problem were a legal
one. Indeed, Ivan Ilyich's legalistic mode—scrutinize, adjudicate,
sentence—is closely analogous to his doctor's medical one—examine,
diagnose, treat—and a good deal more conclusive. 'As he put on airs
before the accused in court,' Ivan Ilyich realizes at his first diagnostic
consultation, 'so the famous doctor put on airs before him ... For Ivan
Ilyich only one question mattered: was his condition dangerous or
not? But the doctor ignored this inappropriate question ... just exactly
what Ivan Ilyich himself had performed as brilliantly a thousand
times over the accused.'

But really the judge's magisterial overview is here the frightened
man's instinctive defence against *un*-control; 'it's *already* much better'.

The point here is not that Ivan Ilyich has lost his mind. It might almost be better if he had. On the contrary, the terrible truth is that Ivan Ilyich is in control of his illness only to the extent that he *can* mentalize it. His condition is tolerably thinkable only so long as he can locate it ('the appendix'); minimize it ('a little thing, a tiny little thing' as small in mind as he makes-believe it is in body); and palpably mend it, by the sheer force of his desire to be well ('I feel *a little, a lot* better').

I choose this novella in part because, as Marilyn J. Field put it in 1997 (when she was on the US National Academy of Sciences Committee on End of Life Care):

It is the one literary work that approaches canonical status in Medical Humanities. It is taught often in US medical schools: were it a short story rather than a novella it probably would be required now for graduation. It is that rare work, an imagined account of the whole process of dying as it happens to one person'.[33]

More recently, the surgeon Atul Gawande, wrote:

I learned about a lot of things in medical school, but mortality wasn't one of them. Although I was given a dry, leathery corpse to dissect in my first term, that was solely a way to learn about human anatomy. Our textbooks had almost nothing on aging or frailty or dying. How the process unfolds, how people experience the end of their lives, and how it affects those around them seemed beside the point. [...] The one time I remember discussing mortality was during an hour we spent on *The Death of Ivan Ilyich* in a weekly seminar called Patient-Doctor.[34]

As this status and influence attests—not only in medical humanities but across the medical profession—*The Death of Ivan Ilyich* offered to practitioners some crucial awareness or dimension that no other discourse they encountered did give or could give. But the main reason for concentrating on this work is that it best exhibits literature's power to go beyond standard norms and defences. Indeed, it makes the greatest possible demands on human thought, in the face of the loss of all that makes for life and health. *The Death of Ivan Ilyich* is a text that has most to deal with the unthinkable, in which dying is at once an impossible thought and a humanly necessary one.

So it is that what must come after Ivan Ilyich's denials is that characteristic Tolstoyan turn where life's brittle surfaces are forced to give way to a deeper reality. Suddenly just when he thinks he can forget it, the old familiar pain returns, 'stubborn, quiet, serious':

> And suddenly he pictured the matter from an entirely different side. 'The appendix! The kidney!' he said to himself. 'This is not a matter of the appendix or the kidney, but of life and...death. Yes, there was life, and now it is going, going, and I cannot hold it back. Yes, why deceive myself? Isn't it obvious to everybody except me that I'm dying and it is only a question of the number of weeks, days – right now maybe.' (Chapter Five)

There is no psychological defence, nothing inside himself, Ivan Ilyich finds, to protect against his 'insides' when they have come so viscerally to determine who he is. But more than that, the naming of those insides—kidney, appendix—and the whole business of medical diagnosis is no defence either.

For the diagnosis of symptoms, the taking of medicines, the search for a cure eventually are not a means of realistically facing the problem but are themselves symptoms of trying to get away from the reality those symptoms deeply represent, existentially. Not 'the appendix! the kidney!' but 'life and...death'. So long as Ivan Ilyich is stuck at this first stage, he is avoiding the next and vital one—the only in which this novella is really concerned: first-order, primary reality, the thing in itself. Here, in the next move of this passage, is where that almost unthinkable reality first fully hits Ivan Ilyich:

> Cold came over him, his breath stopped. He heard only the pounding of his heart.
>
> 'There will be no me, so what will there be? There will be nothing. So where will I be, when there's no me? Can this be death? No, I don't want it.' (Chapter Five)

Moments ago, Ivan Ilyich voluntarily imagined 'absorption, ejection, restoration' of physical functioning; now he is forced to imagine the radically *un*imaginable extinction of that life—nothing, 'no me', not being. Suddenly, mid-paragraph, the prose occupies a 'there, where, when' that is nowhere—a space in which all normal structures of thought or category are suspended or no longer exist.

It is not merely Ivan Ilyich's professional forms which suffer breakdown here, but everything that holds the earth together for mortal thinkers. This existential hiatus produces momentarily the symptoms of physical death: 'Cold came over him. His breath stopped.'

But Ivan Ilyich does not die on the thought of death. On the contrary he *'hears'* his fate in 'the pounding of his heart'; it means the sentient thought of death is the most alive thing in Ivan Ilyich. That is the paradoxical turnaround, in this work which always marks the alternative to straightforward linear thinking in life. Within it is the great challenge and paradox—that the thought of death, and death itself, are not co-terminous, so that death has to *be* a human thought, but a paradoxical one in that it will be the end of all thought for this thinker. It is a space or dimension, where the thought and imagination of being 'nothing' is, for the instant, a possible thought. This novella insists on these terrible thought-spaces all the more for witnessing their exclusion from human norms.

In terms of these norms, at a critical point in his career, Ivan Ilyich missed out for a second time on a promotion:

> Ivan Ilyich felt for the first time not merely boredom but an unbearable anguish, and he decided that it was impossible to live like that, and that it was necessary to take decisive measures.
>
> Having spent a sleepless night, pacing the terrace the whole time, Ivan Ilych decided to go to Petersburg to solicit for himself, and, so as to punish *them* for not knowing how to appreciate him, to transfer to another ministry. (Chapter Three)

'Unbearable...impossible': the painful, dark, demanding territory, where human striving is thrown out of its own story and must bear the 'impossible', is what this novella unstintingly seeks. *But* this is not yet the real thing, precisely because the protagonist can solve this problem, cure this remediable malady. This is what William James called the 'healthy-mindedness' which is a prerequisite of normal bourgeois life.[35] That is why contemporary forms of healthy-mindedness—positive thinking, self-help—very sensibly address just the kind of common mental health issue that threatens Ivan Ilyich: depression occasioned by career disappointment.

Imagine for a moment that we were not reading literature here, but a self-help book. Martin Seligman, the American psychologist who is one of the most successful exponents of positive thinking as a self-help tool, would probably say, in the case of Ivan Ilyich, that he has taken precisely the right steps to prevent one of the acknowledged determiners of depression—helplessness. What Seligman calls 'learnt helplessness' is triggered when a person finds that any response he or she makes in the face of challenge has no impact or bearing upon that situation. This turns into a profoundly debilitating loss of trust in one's capacity to control one's own life:

> If we habitually believe . . . that misfortune is our fault, is enduring and will undermine everything we do, more of it will befall us than if we believe otherwise. . . . When we overestimate our helplessness, other forces will take control. Pessimistic prophecies are self-fulfilling.[36]

If you give in to 'pessimistic explanatory style'—saying 'the bad event in my life is permanent and pervasive', 'Nothing I do matters'—then low mood turns to depression, and depression even to suicide. But instead, Seligman encourages 'learnt optimism': 'You increase your control over the way you think about adversity' not through drugs or counselling but by 'learning a set of skills on how to talk to *yourself* when you suffer a personal defeat'. Positive thinking in this sense— putting 'healthy' thoughts 'in place of' or as support against 'morbid' ones—is actually what Ivan Ilyich has practised all his adult life. It is not only protection against the darkness: it is the way to a version of the good life.

So the result of Ivan Ilyich's decisiveness is what seems to be the crowning achievement of his professional life—the appointment to a highly prestigious judiciary position. But actually again it is not the great moment of his life; dying is. It 'was like what happens on the train, when you think you are moving forward, but are moving backward and suddenly find out the real direction' (Chapter Twelve). For the moment, the train which is The Life of Ivan Ilyich resumes its wonted smooth pathway, without consciousness of representing anything other than resounding success. No wonder he thinks this is progress. Everyone would prefer to cling to secondary forms than admit that they are in fact secondary. This is sensible, normally sensible.

Depression, in Ivan Ilyich's case, as some might say blithely enough, is a missed spiritual opportunity for seeking something other than a goal-oriented life. But of course Ivan Ilyich wants to miss that spiritual opportunity and get his promotion; who wouldn't? He moves on, as we say—and up.

But it is still frightening that this form of thinking is not stupid, is so enticingly sensible. Myself, I do not want to live in a world in which people seek breakdowns. I want to live in a world where people legitimately seek and find protection. But at the same time I do not want a human world where the only good thoughts are about how to get on. Here is what this mended or so-called successful world is like; here is Ivan's world of promotion, as Heidegger describes it:

> Everything that is original is flattened down as something long since known. Everything won through struggle becomes something manageable. Every mystery loses its power. The care of averageness reveals, in turn, an essential tendency...which we call *levelling down* of all possibilities of being. It does not get to the heart of the matter because it is insensitive to every difference of level, genuineness.[37]

Ivan Ilyich is again the man of the norm, of the art of the possible, by fitting in, by going along *with* the grain, doing what he feels he is expected to do. It is only by being thrown free of norm's narrative, forced into a dramatic switch of position—from judge to 'accused'—that Ivan Ilyich is galvanized into seeing *himself* in terms of merely efficient averageness. In such a world real thinking in Bion's crucial sense, true being in Heidegger's, is simply incompatible with living an ordinary 'decent' life, because not thinking is precisely the price paid for staying in and surviving the norm. 'It does not get to the heart of the matter.'

Actually, for Ivan, escape into success is only judgment deferred. That judgment returns now, in illness increasingly seen to be mortal. 'If a man has learned to think, no matter what he may think about, he is always thinking of his own death,' said Tolstoy.[38]

> He called up a series of other thoughts in place of this thought, in hopes of finding support in them. He tried to go back to his former ways of thinking, which had screened him formerly

> from the thought of death. But – strange thing – all that had
> formerly screened, hidden, wiped out the consciousness of
> death now could no longer produce that effect. Lately Ivan
> Ilyich had spent most of his time in these attempts to restore the
> former ways of feeling that had screened him from death.
> (Chapter Six)

'Strange thing', perhaps the very strangest—Ivan Ilyich cannot consciously think this terrible truth nor can he *not* think it either. Ivan
Ilyich has not only not thought about his own death: he has learned
an alternative or substitutive mode of thought—a mode which I shall
call 'learnt non-thinking'. The function of this mode is to screen, hide,
wipe out from consciousness just those areas of human experience for
which human beings, says Bion, have developed a capacity to think at
all. Tolstoy's more ultimate, ancient vision is perhaps more crucial
than ever in starkly revealing the dangers of a quick-fix life cure that
can seem so benignly easy, comfortable and available, and which, in
both its method and its appeal, is neither designed nor equipped to
challenge individual and cultural default modes. And yet Tolstoy's
own vision is testimony to the degree to which humans are evolved to
do the easy, not the strange thing—until every conceivable resource of
adaptation runs out:

> In the depths of his soul Ivan Ilyich knew that he was dying, but
> not only was he not accustomed to it, he simply did not, he
> could not possibly understand it. [...]
>   'It can't be. It can't be, but it is. How can it be? How can I
> understand it?'
>   And he could not understand and tried to drive this thought
> away as false, incorrect, morbid and to dislodge it with other cor-
> rect healthy thoughts. But this thought, not only a thought but as
> if a reality, came back again and stood before him. (Chapter Six)

'He could not possibly understand [понял]' is this novella's terrifying
discovery. I quote the Russian here to show that the very same verb
and faculty which for Levin was the crucial enabler in the challenge of
life—'Now he understood [понял] for the first time'—is rendered, at
the point of death, Ivan Ilyich's greatest disability. But all that any-
body can bring to such understanding are the tools for thinking which

have served them so far in life. *The Death of Ivan Ilyich* shows that humans are least adapted to think about that most common and inevitable thing—their own death. The objective truth of death cannot be borne subjectively, says Thomas Nagel: the two modes will not go together; we cannot take in the objective and carry on the same.[39] Yet in Ivan Ilyich at this moment, the impossibility of thinking at one level he will die, as well as the obviousness of it at another, are held unsquareably together—'It can't be. It can't be,' he says, then adds immediately, 'but it is'. More, this thought was 'not only a thought *but as if a reality*': the man thinks of this ultimate reality; but this is a reality so powerful, so absolute, that it breaks the thought that tries to contain it. The reality is bigger than the thought, even as the reality temporarily dwells in the thought, realizes it. Reality explodes. It is a happening so frighteningly vertiginous as to be itself barely thinkable: to think of death; to think of death entering this thought; to think that what I am thinking of is far less real than the reality it tries and fails to encapsulate. This is what is meant in this present book by 'literary thinking': not something arcane or aesthetic, but something that is of the human, comes from it, belongs to it, but which—like 'I will die'—can hardly be contained within it. There is the screen of the norm. But then there is the final screen—thought itself, when one supposes that thinking can truly describe or wholly control the reality it is thinking of. This is the *really real*, the essential truth, Bion's 0, Tolstoy's 'it'. It is more than logic:

> Caius is a man, men are mortal, therefore Caius is mortal - had seemed to him all his life to be correct only in relation to Caius, but by no means to himself. [...] And Caius is indeed mortal, and it's right that he die, but for me, little Vanya, Ivan Ilyich, with all my thoughts and emotions – for me it's another matter. [...] 'How can it be? How can I understand it?' (Chapter Six)

Professional logic is especially redundant here. Yet literary realism's domain is precisely that area where the objective *turns into* the subjective, the point when, as George Eliot puts it, 'the commonplace "We all must die"' transforms itself suddenly into the acute consciousness "I must die" (*Middlemarch,* Chapter Forty-two), and the merely real becomes the really real.

At such moments, literary language supplants the language of logic in order to do the necessary superhuman thinking beyond normal category—to have the thought which no human could have within ordinary life and survive it. The novel, as a language and form of thinking was, for Tolstoy, the one authentic alternative to rational secular philosophy:

> [The philosophers] seemed fruitful to him when he read...But he had only to refer back from life itself to what had satisfied him while he thought along a given line – and suddenly the whole artificial edifice would collapse like a house of cards, and it would be clear that the edifice had been made [...] without regard for something more important in life than reason. (*Anna Karenina*, Book Eight, Chapter Nine)

****

This goes for other well-meaning forms of normal thinking. A recent medical trainee journal discussing *The Death of Ivan Ilyich*, concentrates on the figure of Gerasim, the uneducated peasant servant who supports Ivan Ilyich, even with physical literalness—holding the sick man's legs 'sometimes all night long'—but chiefly in this respect: 'Gerasim alone did not lie; everything showed that he alone understood what it was all about, and did not find it necessary to conceal it, and simply pitied his emaciated, weakened master.... "We'll all die, why not take trouble?"' Gerasim is offered to medical students as an 'encouraging' model of 'empathy' and of how 'to be real' in the face of death.[40] Behind such readings is a valuable intuition of the doctor's potential role as witness to individual suffering. It seems almost churlish and somehow ungrateful, as well as contradictory of the aims and argument of this book, to be critical of those many medical practitioners and teachers who find in *The Death of Ivan Ilyich*, even thus instrumentally, something they practically and humanly need.[41]

But I am critical, even if I could do no better myself. For this reading misses something crucial in the light of Gerasim's role in this critical episode. Ivan is coming out of a terrible nightmare of dying—a nightmare which on waking seems deeper than the daylight world:

> The same Gerasim is sitting at the foot of the bed, dozing calmly, patiently. And he is lying with his emaciated legs in

stockings placed on Gerasim's shoulders; the same candle with its shade, and the same unceasing pain.

'Go away Gerasim,' he whispered.

'Never mind, I'll stay, sir.'

'No, go away.'

He took his legs down, lay sideways on his arm, and felt sorry for himself. He waited only until Gerasim went to the next room, and then stopped holding himself back and wept like a child. He wept over his helplessness, over his terrible loneliness, over the cruelty of people, over the cruelty of God, over the absence of God. [...] Then he quieted down, not only stopped weeping, but stopped breathing, and became all attention: it was as if he were listening not to a voice that spoke in sounds, but to the voice of his soul, to the course of thoughts arising in him.

'What do you want?' was the first clear idea, expressible in words, that he heard. 'What do you want? What do you want?' he repeated to himself. (Chapter Nine)

Ivan Ilyich is at his most vulnerably and emotionally real only *after* Gerasim has gone—at the very moment he is sent away; '*then*' he 'wept like a child'. Everything that Gerasim has supported externally in the very stolidity of his physical being—pity, recognition— now have to be suffered alone by Ivan Ilyich. As Ivan Ilyich, not someone else, has to do the dying, so Ivan Ilyich, and not someone else, must do the accepting. 'Go away' is Ivan Ilyich's final dismissal of the whole outer life. And it is critical that he dismisses not just its falsity but its goodness and truth too, since, embodied in Gerasim, these constitute the greater temptation here. The servant's witnessing presence gets in the way of the truth waiting to be found within Ivan Ilyich himself. Reading this passage with an MA English Literature class for mature postgraduate students—a mix of health, education, and other professionals– we were struck by the repeated word at the close of the first paragraph 'The *same* Gerasim...the *same* candle...the *same* unceasing pain'. 'But Ivan Ilyich is not the same,' said one student. 'He's on *the other side*'. That is a big clue as to what is at stake in reading *The Death of Ivan Ilyich*. For, from hereon, Ivan Ilyich has gone beyond all forms of conventional human care. And his being thus beyond human help, as we come to see, is emphatically not the same as helplessness.

Yet this does not mean that Gerasim's actions are to be scorned. On the contrary, the value of Gerasim's genuineness as a model for medics, as well as the great human achievement it represents, is best illustrated by comparison with Levin's involuntary failures in this regard, when, in the prime of a life devoted vigorously to managing the old family estate, he is visited by his dying brother Nikolai:

> He had just partly clarified the question of how to live, when he was presented with a new insoluble problem – death.
>
> So he's dying, so he'll die towards spring, so how can I help him? What can I say to him? What do I know about it? I even forgot there was such a thing.'...
>
> Levin felt himself guilty and could do nothing about it. He felt that if they both had not pretended but had spoken, as the phrase goes, from the heart – that is, only what they both actually thought and felt – they would have looked into each other's eyes, and Konstantin would have said only, 'You're going to die, to die, to die!' and Nikolai would have answered only, 'I know I'm going to die, but I'm afraid, afraid, afraid!' And they would have said nothing else if they had spoken from the heart. But it was impossible to live that way, and therefore Konstantin tried to do what he had tried to do all his life without succeeding, and what in his observation, many could do so well, and without which it was impossible to live: he tried to say what he did not think, and kept feeling that it came out false, that his brother noticed it and was annoyed by it. (*Anna Karenina*, Book Three, Chapter Thirty-two)

The honest near-comic bafflement registered within the protagonist is that honesty itself is 'impossible' here: the polite lie is unavoidable, even though it is an offence against truth as it exists for his dying brother. The obdurate complication for relatives of the dying is that death places these loved ones in separate worlds, even while they remain and belong together in the same close family. They might almost want to say: 'You're going to die, to die, to die!', the dying one might almost want to reply 'I know...I'm afraid, afraid, afraid!' But it isn't said—except that the novel says it, subterraneously, in some shared world which is existent in this scene if not made articulate. And the great unspoken reality here is not only death but love. Because the novel's language dares and bears to keep faith even with what is wrong or missed in the situation itself, it registers the closeness that helps redeem the separation in a way that the brothers themselves cannot quite. The novel speaks for the heart more honestly than the heart of either Konstantin or Nikolai can manage—truth's witness in lieu of a Gerasim.

The Death of Ivan Ilyich is about nothing less than the absolute impossible. At the last, his young son movingly holds Ivan's hand to say he is not alone.

He indicated his son to his wife with his eyes and said:

> 'Take him away…sorry…for you, too…' He also wanted to say 'Forgive,' but said 'Forgo,' and, no longer able to correct himself, waved his hand, knowing that the one who had to would understand. (Chapter Twelve)

Here the boy replaces Gerasim. '[Ivan Ilyich] responds to his son's gesture, feels pity for his family and so triumphs over death', says Marilyn Field.[42] Psychiatrist and medical humanities Professor Robert Coles concludes: 'As [Ivan Ilyich] died he was born – he became for the first time someone who could reach out, connect with others'.[43] The key problem with such decent and sensible humanist paraphrases is that no paraphrase could ever be commensurate with this instant of reality. 'The moment the conditions for 0 do not exist […] any formulation felt to approximate to illumination of 0 is certain to produce an obstructive rigidity'.[44] That is why Bion calls reality '0', knowing that no ordinary language will serve. Any attempted formulation—my own included, as I find this almost impossible to write *about*—appears dry and residual since it must by definition stay stubbornly on 'this side', the norm of externalized description when it is the norm itself that is being breached here. The extra reality comes with this clause, this thought—'the one who had to would understand': it does not just break the normalistic frame; it breaks with finite frames altogether. It is faith in some 'one' which makes the impossible thought possible. What is 'the one'? 'Is it God?' asks a member of the MA group. 'Could it be the reader?' ventures another. But we all feel these 'answers' are too specific, too easy. ' "The one who *had to*…" ' Does this mean Ivan

Ilyich *doesn't* have to know his son or wife understand any more?'
These are not answers, they are gestures which point to the right place
without knowing why it is right. It is why the sensible medical humanities approach simply will not do here. The experience must not be
used—only *let be*, in *its* words. You cannot say it, and certainly not
better than Tolstoy, but you can keep pointing to it and trying to let its
broken syllables get mouthed.

It is important now only to know what is wrong, what this particular
experience is *not*. It is not what we might have expected—the bitter-
ness of Jude the Obscure's 'Too late, too late for me' or Lear's 'never,
never, never, never, never.' It is not too late, suddenly, and it does not
matter at this ultimate level of reality if no one around seems to know
it. There is 'the one who had to' who 'would understand'; a faith that
this truth creates its own reality, that a truth is never too late, never
without a recognizer. It is the impossible made suddenly possible in
this tale that comes back from the dead to tell itself. The story opens a
portal, a thought space where the breaking through of the infinite into
the finite happens every time the tale is read.

'If I were to try to say in words,' Tolstoy wrote of *Anna Karenina*,
'everything that I intended to express in my novel, I would have to
write the same novel I wrote from the beginning'.[45] What Tolstoy's
statement really means is that the novel exists in resistance to a language of explanation which would be disloyal to its reality. It is the
Tolstoyan equivalent to Bion's dictum that 0 cannot be contained
within any theory about it. 'In mathematics, calculations can be made
without the presence of the objects about which calculation is necessary'.[46] But elsewhere it cannot be so. One definition of literary thinking, I propose, might be this: that literature can 'think' reality when
ordinary human thought falls short; that a book can have thoughts
that humans *cannot* have.

Notes

1. Wilfred R. Bion, *Experiences in Groups*, 1961 (London: Routledge, 1994), pp. 22,
   89–91, 151–4.
2. Wilfred R. Bion, *Learning from Experience* (London: Maresfield Library, 1962), p. 84.
3. Wilfred R. Bion, *Second Thoughts* (London: Maresfield Library, 1967), p. 117.
4. Wilfred R. Bion, *Learning from Experience* (London: Maresfield Library, 1962), p. 56.
5. Wilfred R. Bion, *Learning from Experience* (London: Maresfield Library, 1962), pp. 42, 56.

6. Sigmund Freud, 'Formulations on the Two Principles of Mental Functioning', 1911, Penguin Freud Library, Vol. 11 (Harmondsworth, Middlesex: Penguin Books Ltd, 1991), pp. 35–6.

7. Adam Phillips, Introduction to *The Penguin Freud Reader* (London: Penguin Books Ltd, 2006), p. xii.

8. Wilfred R. Bion, *Attention and Interpretation* (London: Maresfield Library, 1970), p. 26.

9. Wilfred R. Bion, *Transformations: Change from Learning to Growth* (London: Heinemann, 1965), p. 148.

10. Wilfred R. Bion, *Second Thoughts* (London: Maresfield Library, 1967), p. 141; *Attention and Interpretation* (London: Maresfield Library, 1970), p. 107.

11. Wilfred R. Bion, *Learning from Experience* (London: Maresfield Library, 1962), p. 93.

12. Wilfred R. Bion, *Second Thoughts* (London: Maresfield Library, 1967), p. 112.

13. Wilfred R. Bion, *Learning from Experience* (London: Maresfield Library, 1962), p. 57.

14. George Eliot, *Middlemarch*, 1871–2, Chapter Twenty.

15. Charles Darwin, *The Expression of the Emotions in Man and Animals*, 1872 (London: HarperCollins, 1998), pp. 157–8.

16. Wilfred R. Bion, *Learning from Experience* (London: Maresfield Library, 1962), p. 35.

17. Benedictus de Spinoza, *Ethics*, 1677, translated by George Eliot (Salzburg: University of Salzburg, 1981), pp. 93, 219–20, 229.

18. Richard Pevear and Larissa Volokhonsky, trans. *Anna Karenina* (London: Penguin Books Ltd, 2003).

19. Wilfred R. Bion, *Attention and Interpretation* (London: Maresfield Library, 1970), p. 9.

20. Wilfred R. Bion, *Attention and Interpretation* (London: Maresfield Library, 1970), p. 11.

21. Wilfred R. Bion, *Learning from Experience* (London: Maresfield Library, 1962), p. 83.

22. Wilfred R. Bion, *Attention and Interpretation* (London: Maresfield Library, 1970), pp. 11–12.

23. Søren Kierkegaard, *The Sickness Unto Death*, 1849, trans Alastair Hannay (Harmondsworth, Middlesex: Penguin Books Ltd, 1989), pp. 81–4.

24. D. H. Lawrence, 'Study of Thomas Hardy', 1936, in *Study of Thomas Hardy and Other Essays* (Cambridge: Cambridge University Press, 1988), p. 30.

25. Raymond Williams, *Modern Tragedy* (London: Chatto and Windus, 1966), p. 129.

26. Wilfred R. Bion, *Attention and Interpretation* (London: Maresfield Library, 1970), p. 106.

27. Leo Tolstoy, *Complete Works*, ed. M.B. Hrapchenko, 22 vols (Moscow: Khudozhestvennaia, 1978–85), vol. 11, p. 65.

28. Online Dialectical Behavioural Course, Emotion Regulation/Emotion Regulation for the Holidays http://www.dbtselfhelp.com/html/holidays.html (accessed 26 March 2016).

29. Henri Bergson, *Creative Evolution*, 1911 (New York: Dover Publications Inc, 1998), p. 240.

30. Immanuel Kant, *Critique of Pure Reason* (1788), A51–2, B75–6.

31. George Henry Lewes, *Problems of Life and Mind* (London: Trubner and Co., 1875), pp. 412–15.

32. This translation is by Rosemary Edmonds: see Leo Tolstoy, *The Death of Ivan Ilyich and Other Stories* (Penguin Books Ltd: Harmondsworth, Middlesex, 1960).

33. Marilyn J. Field and Christine K. Cassell (eds) *Approaching Death: Improving Care at the End of Life* (Washington D.C.: National Academy Press, 1997), p. 2.

34. Atul Gawande, *Being Mortal: Aging, Illness, Medicine and What Matters in the End* (London: Profile Books Ltd, 2014), p. 1.

35. William James, *The Varieties of Religious Experience*, 1902 (Harmondsworth, Middlesex: Penguin Books Ltd), p. 162.

36. Martin E. P. Seligman, *Learned Optimism: How to Change Your Mind and Life* (New York: Vintage Books, 1990), pp. 7, 76, 207, 283.

37. Martin Heidegger, *Being and Time*, 1953 (New York: SUNY Press), p. 123.

38. Maxim Gorky, 'A Letter', Reminiscences of Leo Nikolaevich Tolstoy, translated by S. S. Koteliansky and Leonard Woolf, 1920 (Adelaide: University of Adelaide, 2014).

39. Thomas Nagel, *The View from Nowhere* (Oxford: Oxford University Press, 1986), p. 225.

40. Blake Charlton, Abrahan Verghese, 'Caring for Ivan Ilyich', *Journal of General Intern Medicine*, Jan 2010, 25(1): 93–5.

41. One key lesson the work teaches, says a recent clinical symposium on end of life issues ('*The Death of Ivan Ilyich*: A Blueprint for Intervention at End of Life', 2011), is the crucial importance of honesty of diagnosis in supporting the patient in the classic stages from denial to acceptance (as established in Elizabeth Kubler-Ross's *On Death and Dying*, 1969). The value of this novella in medical training is more practical than the latter text, Warren Lee Holleman has argued, in that 'it help[s] students understand how patients die, what helps, and what hurts, so as to prepare them for their hospital rotations', 'Death education in American medical schools: Tolstoy's challenge to Kübler-Ross', *Journal of Medical Humanities*, March 1991, 12(1); pp. 11–18, p. 5.

42. Marilyn J. Field and Christine K. Cassell (eds), *Approaching Death: Improving Care at the End of Life* (Washington D.C.: National Academy Press, 1997), p. 2.

43. Robert Coles, *The Call of Stories: Teaching and the Moral Imagination* (Boston: Houghton Mifflin, 1989), p. 167.

44. Wilfred R. Bion, *Attention and Interpretation* (London: Maresfield Library, 1970), p. 81.

45. R. F. Christian (ed & trans), *Tolstoy's Letters*, 2 vols (London: Athlone Press), vol. 1, p. 296.

46. Wilfred R. Bion, *Attention and Interpretation* (London: Maresfield Library, 1970), p. 81.

2

Telling a New Story

Literary Narrative and Narrative Medicine

In Favour of Story

Christopher Dowrick, my Liverpool colleague, a professor of primary care and himself a GP, describes in *Beyond Depression* a visit to his surgery from Ian, a retired British Army restaurateur with three grown-up children, whose heavy drinking is exacerbating his diabetes and high blood pressure and who, more recently, has been suffering blackouts. He is sleeping badly, often irritable, rarely goes out of the house and is alarmed to find he can no longer be bothered to see his children. He puts his situation in simple common language: 'You see doc, basically the problem for me is I just can't see any point in getting up in the morning any more':

> He talks about his loss of ability, his painful feet and the complications of his diabetes, present and to come. He talks about his loss of purpose, how he used to be a good restaurateur and a good father but he has no role in either arena now. All he can see now is a slow, inexorable path toward death. His problem now seems to me to be beyond the reach of medicine and to go way beyond the reach of any formal diagnosis. Ian and I are facing a profound existential question: what, actually, is the point in his being alive?[1]

In an everyday routine surgery, this GP deals here not with the absolute pain of death but with the pain that does *not* kill while it can surely defeat all sense of purpose in going on living. In place of the increasing certainty of death which confronted Ivan Ilyich, this patient faces the insupportable prospect of a continued but apparently worthless life. The man no longer has a function or occupation, as father or restaurateur; he has no purpose to make every morning part of a life story rather than just a matter of time after time. As Dowrick recognizes, such suffering no longer fits into the body as a mere symptom, nor into the world as a medical diagnosis. What we call depression is perhaps really the name we give to the problem of a person outliving his or her sense of 'fitting', or never having had a place or form.

What is humanly required in such situations is precisely a *general* practitioner, one who, by contrast with the medical specialist, is prepared to see beyond what specialist medicine alone can offer. Generalism, here, means taking seriously the human trouble which does not have a ready name or diagnosis. It is a willingness to enter the inchoate and indeterminate areas of individual experience where technical efficiency and skill alone are out of place or redundant.

It was creation of the hospital in the nineteenth century that began increasingly to give rise to the specialist consultant. The pressure of large numbers of patients had introduced, into an urgently required system of collectivized care, a new emphasis on finding the common characteristics of the same disease in different people, in order to identify, through systematic biomedical experiment, the most widely effective treatment. These advances are of course, as I have said earlier, sensible and admirable, part of the necessary systematization and specialization of processes for which we are all at various times most grateful, and which bring much relief to suffering. Increasingly, even so, the expert physician's commitment to diagnostic classification and scientific objectivity made him or her a specialist in respect of the *disease*, not the patient. But for the traditional family doctor, whose role hospital medicine began to replace, the reverse had been true; before the availability of sophisticated technology such as stethoscopes and thermometers for physical examination, a doctor's practice was based entirely upon an intimate knowledge of patients' circumstances. Though under severe time pressure with fifteen-minute appointment slots, the modern GP may still be able at best to continue this humane tradition, remaining close to communities, and observing illness within the particular life contexts.

Yet, as biomedicine has made its enormous technical advances, seeking to fit the full range of presenting symptoms to clinical taxonomies which explain, treat and cure them, today's GP, almost paradoxically, is a generalist *against the grain*. More specialists has meant more diagnoses, and more diagnoses has meant that more people previously considered relatively normal and healthy are included within the definition of treatable or preventable disease. At the same time, the demise of religious and philosophical justification for the sheer arbitrariness of human suffering has made illness one of the few validated expressions of unhappiness. In these circumstances, says Iona Heath, former President of the Royal College of Physicians, a GP is tasked with 'holding the border' between a subjective sense of illness and scientific disease categories where there exists 'the huge undifferentiated burden of human distress'. There the indeterminacy of illness that specialists cannot easily categorize also makes for the benign indeterminacy of doctorly function.

Heath worked as an inner city GP in North London for thirty-five years. As writer and editor for the *British Medical Journal* and as executive member of the World Organization of Family Doctors, she has campaigned tirelessly in her writing and in her public roles for the kind of humane and holistic approach to health care which her own everyday practice has always instinctively embodied. Her decision to become a GP was confirmed by her unhappy experience of hospital rotations as a trainee: 'I realized I like to see people in their own clothes and homes rather than the way they become depersonalized in hospital, however hard you try.'[2] Her long experience in general practice has taught that the doctor's first task and duty is very simply to listen to the patient's vulnerably uncertain sense of 'something being wrong'.

> The words well up, not from a standardized bodily object defined by biology, but direct from the symptoms of a unique human subject created by biography. Lives wound bodies and wounds leave deep bodily scars that never fully heal. Patients' presentation of their symptoms *emerge* rather than *result* from their experience of the symptoms themselves.[3]

It is this primary personal data—the patient's raw expression of deeply felt unhealed wounds—upon which the doctor must first rely, not in place of effective care but in order the more accurately and usefully to provide it. If the untidy symptoms do not fit the medical theory, it is the theory that has to be revised or discounted, not the patient's experience. 'Doctors need always to remember that what the patient feels is the reality on which they must base their practice.'[4] This is what 'primary care' really means here.

Heath's account of the vital importance of personal biography is at once a description and a defence of the rationale of what has become known as narrative-based medicine, as it is practised in the US and UK today. Fundamentally, narrative medicine seeks the reorientation of the doctor's attention toward the person, not the pain. A patient such as Ian has only symptoms to point to, and, in a secular world, only a doctor to turn to. The doctor, in such circumstances, is as much pastor as medic, and is listening to a personal story, not just a list of presenting symptoms preparatory to producing a patient record. More than anything else, says Arthur Kleinman, an early pioneer of narrative medicine, it is the separation of the illness from its sufferer in the modern transformation of the medical care system, that has alienated the ill from their professional caregivers and the latter from the ancient reward of the profession—the capacity to do good for another. Chronic illness like Ian's is not only inseparable from a life history: it actually *is* still a life, its embodied experience. Caring for the patient's story is not a peripheral task but constitutes the very point of medicine.[5]

What is more, the patient himself or herself cannot do without a sense of story. 'To be ourselves we must *have* ourselves – possess, if need be re-possess, our life-stories' says Oliver Sacks.[6] An extreme example dramatizes what is nonetheless commonly important. In 'The Lost Mariner', Sacks gives an account of Jimmie, an intelligent and high functioning forty-nine-year-old man whose memory of his life had stopped, thirty years earlier, in 1945. His psycho-neurological disorder was caused in part by the trauma of being discharged from the navy; without purposeful work and habitual structure he had 'gone to pieces'. It was also the result of the heavy drinking and severe alcoholism that followed. Jimmie's condition meant that he had vivid and affectionate recollection of his boyhood and naval service as a radio operator on submarines, but no memory of anything following, including the very recent past. 'He is a man without a past (or future), stuck in a constantly changing meaningless moment: a pit into which everything, every experience, every event, would fathomlessly drop.'

Sacks hoped the man himself might not be aware of his own lack of continuity:

> 'How do you feel?'
>
> 'How do I feel,' he repeated, and scratched his head. 'I cannot say I feel ill. But I cannot say I feel well. I cannot say I feel anything at all.'
>
> 'Are you miserable?' I continued.
>
> 'Can't say I am.'
>
> 'Do you enjoy life?'
>
> 'I can't say I do...'
>
> I hesitated, fearing that I was going too far, that I might be stripping a man down to some hidden, unacknowledgeable, unbearable despair.
>
> 'You don't enjoy life,' I repeated, hesitating somewhat. 'How then *do* you feel about life?'
>
> 'I can't say that I feel anything at all.'
>
> 'You feel alive though?'
>
> 'Feel alive? Not really. I haven't felt alive for a very long time.'

His face wore a look of infinite sadness and resignation.[7] For Sacks, the litmus test for ascertaining whether Jimmie actually experiences his own suffering is the capacity to feel intensely. What he finds instead is the feeling of *not feeling anything*, of not even feeling alive, in the absence of a story to make life or feeling *matter* to the man in any way. Not to know one's own story—'the inner narrative whose sense *is* our lives' (p. 105)—is the deepest and saddest illness of all. In *Permanent Present Tense*, Suzanne Corkin tells the story of Henry Gustave Molaison who at the age of twenty-seven underwent a psychosurgical procedure that went disastrously wrong, leaving him without long-term memory. He had to have written on a piece of paper the fact that his father had died to explain to him his vague sense of unhappiness at times. 'He often asked when his mother and father were coming to visit him.... One of our lab members noticed that he had written two notes to himself, which he kept in his wallet, one saying "Dad's gone", and the other "Mom's in nursing home – in good health" '.[8] The notes protected him from the anxiety of not knowing.

It was the GP and psychotherapist, Michael Balint who above all, in the 1950s, recognized that the patient case-history could be a powerfully tangible tool in reshaping the expert-dependent scientific model of evidence-based diagnosis. Balint was a Hungarian Jew, the son of a physician, who completed medical studies himself in Budapest before becoming a leading figure in psychoanalysis. In 1938, when political conditions made it impossible for Balint to practise, he and his wife emigrated to England. Balint's parents remained in Hungary, committing suicide to avoid capture by the Nazis in 1944.

Balint's work is acknowledged by all key protagonists in the narrative movement in medical care as a prior, even founding, practical model. The famous 'Balint groups' brought together GPs once a week over several years to discuss their everyday practice by looking together at a series of patient histories. The experiment is recorded in Balint's seminal work, *The Doctor, His Patient and the Illness*, first published in 1957. The chief aim of this work was remedial: to ascertain 'certain processes within the doctor–patient relationship . . . which caused both the patient and the doctor unnecessary suffering'.[9] Specifically, Balint was concerned with the common situation resulting from the lack of a simple cure; the doctor responsibly makes a priority of locating an organic foundation to the patient's problem; examinations often prove negative or inconclusive; the patient becomes more fearful and helpless at not being able to name the illness; the doctor feels guilty at not being able to bring relief to the patient.

What Balint saw were individuals who, being socially isolated in anonymous city settings, were increasingly prone to visit the doctor not just with physical complaints but also 'to complain'. 'I have deliberately left the verb without an object, because at this initial stage we do not know which is the more important, the act of complaining or the complaints that are complained of' (*Balint*, p. 2). The ancient meaning of complaining is not of course to do with customer service but lamentations of sorrow that cry out *because* they cannot be cured. Meanwhile, GPs were gaining increased access to powerful diagnostic and investigative facilities, such as thermometers and stethoscopes, providing quick and effective explanations for these complaints. While such speed might sometimes answer to the patient's vulnerable need for their problem to be named and diagnosed, there was an attendant risk that such solutions could leave the patient's 'deep burning problems' unexpressed and unresolved.

The doctors who attended the discussion groups provided recent case histories, presenting concrete clinical observations of individual patients. But they were encouraged from the beginning to include as full an account as possible of their emotional responses to the patient and the patient's problem. 'At the outset, I had some idea that, psychologically, much more happens in general practice between patient and doctor than is discussed in the traditional text books' (*Balint*, pp. 2–3). The longitudinal case histories, often following the development of a case over two or three years, combined clinical testimony with moving personal biography. As Iona Heath, who was herself a Balint group member in the 1970s, powerfully observes: 'For many patients the general practice record . . . is the only sustained concrete documentation of their lives'.[10]

One doctor, for example, provided the case history of Peter, a young man in his twenties, who, married for three weeks, suddenly began to suffer headaches so severe he was unable to walk, and had to be admitted to hospital as an emergency case. The symptoms recurred a year and a half later when his wife also began visiting the doctor with what appeared to be fertility problems. The doctor's interpretation was that neither Peter's symptom nor the timing were arbitrary. Peter's mother had died when he was three and, his father being an invalid and blind, Peter and his two elder brothers were sent to an orphanage, where Peter was neglected and bullied by his siblings. On leaving the orphanage at fourteen, and from then until adulthood, Peter became sole carer to his disabled and demanding father. The sudden onset of Peter's headaches happened, therefore, when for the first time in his life, Peter, as a married man, was no longer pushed around, was free of near-intolerable burdens and, above all, had had his own disregarded need for love finally met. The way Peter experienced his headaches—'pain behind the eyes', the feeling of 'something wrong with the brain'—was really, the GP concluded, a kind of atoning symptom, closely associated with his father's needs, for the colossal guilt of his new-found happiness. Recurrence of the symptoms when his wife wished to have a child was an involuntary sign that Peter was still convalescing from the appalling emotional privations of his own childhood and adolescence, and was himself desperately needy and immature. He was unable to tolerate the prospect of becoming a father himself or of sharing everything with a child. Thus can the medical history bear witness to how a single, definite, generically common symptom can have compressed within it the pain and need of an entire individual life. More, it was the doctor's communicated understanding, and the patient's reciprocal recognition, of the meaning of these symptoms which, in time, helped Peter to overcome them, where the standard treatment, codeine, had made no difference. The next entry of the case history records the birth of a child (*Balint*, pp. 138–48).

The crucial finding which emerged from the experimental Balint groups was that the doctor's responses to the patient often affected the very form of the illness from which the patient suffered.

> By far the most frequently used drug in general practice was the doctor himself. It was not only the bottle of medicine or the box of pills that mattered, but the way the doctor gave them to his patient – in fact, the whole *atmosphere* in which the drug was given and taken. (*Balint*, p. 1)

Since patients benefit from many varieties of 'the drug doctor', the doctor has to be allowed great freedom in practising according to his or her individuality. But a good 'atmosphere'—one which makes for the best possibilities for effective therapy—will always involve the doctor's responding to the patient's need to be taken seriously. This means holding back on giving either a prematurely definite physical diagnosis or a negative finding ('nothing wrong'). The key principle is that 'the doctor must not be in a hurry' and, above all, 'must not get ahead of his patient *emotionally*'. The atmosphere has to be one in which patient and doctor can 'grow together into a better knowledge of one another', tacitly 'bound thenceforth by tenuous, not strictly speaking medical grounds'.

This deep personal understanding is, for Balint, the essential element too often missing in the traditional physician–patient relationship. 'The technique of medical history-taking amounts to a systematic questionnaire. Unfortunately no such systematic questionnaire exists yet in the field of the pathology of the whole person, the true field of general practice':

> It is still doubtful whether it is possible to develop such a system in this field, especially for the 'unorganised' stages of an

illness.... Our experience has invariably been that, *if the doctor asks questions in the manner of medical history-taking, he will always get answers—but hardly anything more.* Before he can arrive at what we call 'deeper diagnosis', he has to learn to *listen.* During the process he will soon find out that there are no straightforward direct questions which could bring to light the kind of information for which he is looking. [emphasis in original]

By 'unorganised', Balint means that stage of the illness where patients 'first create and grow the illness on their own, out of themselves'. Patients consult doctors, he felt, only when they have subconsciously converted their struggle with a problem into an illness about which they feel able to complain. Complaining about the actual problem may have been too shameful, embarrassing, unpleasant, frightening, painful. The doctor's task is to listen for the original problem in place of which the patient offered an illness. The middle-aged man with vertigo is unhappy in marriage; the mother who suffers recurrent sore throats and has a mildly asthmatic child feels lonely and helpless; the adolescent girl with an unsightly skin rash and swelling of the legs has been caring long-term for a seriously ill parent. This kind of listening is very different from history-taking.

> History-taking is concerned almost exclusively with objective events or with events that can easily be expressed in words; and towards such events, both doctor and patients can adopt a detached 'scientific-objective' attitude. The events we are concerned with are highly subjective and personal, often hardly conscious, also, as often as not, there exists no unequivocal way of describing them in words. Nevertheless these events exist and, moreover, they profoundly influence one's life.

These powerful hidden events constitute the 'more' which standardized questions can never elicit because this human matter often does not have substantial, expressible or easily tolerable reality for the patients themselves. What is really being demanded by patients when they visit the doctor is permitted space for 'the sincere opening up of a life, with all its miseries, petty and profound fears, frustrated hopes, few and often very precarious joys'. The patient must speak in his or her own way and, crucially, in his or her own time, such that there

'grows', in place of an illness, an inner momentum powerful enough
to overcome the protective resistances of embarrassment or shame.
The doctor must speak 'only when something is really expected from
him—not prescribing "the right way", but opening possibilities for the
patient to discover some right way for themselves'. But the doctor's
tactful witnessing presence is nonetheless vital to helping the patient
'*realize* his or her *real* problems'. It is because medicine tries to *ignore*
these problems of the apparently undiagnosable or incurable, says
Balint, that a great deal of further, needless suffering has spoiled the
doctor-patient relationship. What the effective doctor essentially gives
to the patient is the atmosphere in which the 'really real' can authentically emerge. It is no accident or surprise that Balint was a pupil
of Wilfred Bion when he first trained at the Tavistock Clinic in
the 1940s.[11]

Balint's legacy to narrative medicine, as it emerged in the final
quarter of the twentieth century in the UK and the US, was essentially twofold. Firstly, his practical and theoretical model encouraged
into general practice the tradition and skills of psychotherapy.
Hitherto, psychotherapy had been the only area of health in which
talking and listening were understood to be an intrinsic part of diagnosis and treatment. In that context, there has always been a close
procedural relation between narrative and psychotherapy. The patient
brings to treatment an incomplete or incomprehensible story and the
therapist assists in reconstructing the underlying unconscious elements or what is missing from the half-known narrative. For Balint,
the GP who remains true to his or her calling as family doctor, has an
incomparable advantage over the psychotherapist because of the
close, constant contact and much wider range of possible relations
with the patient. At any moment, the GP can switch from being medical advisor to being counsellor, neighbour or friend. 'Listening for
right answers' need not be confined to a formal consultation but can
be a continuous process and extend over a lifetime.

Secondly and crucially, Balint's work showed that the doctor's
account of the patient was itself indispensable human evidence,
though not in the way evidence was often calculated. It is this key
recognition that was picked up by the founders of narrative medicine
in the last quarter of the twentieth century. One decisive impetus
to the narrative movement in the 1970s and 1980s was the rise in

evidence-based medicine, and, most especially, of the Randomized Controlled Trial (RCT). 'Evidence', in RCTs, is derived from systematically collected data and large population samples, with the aim of deducing epidemiological laws and maximally applicable treatment methods. The RCT is a scientific experiment, in which the people being studied are randomly allocated either to the particular treatment to be tested, or to a control group where no treatment or a previously tested treatment is administered, so that the two groups can be compared. This method is now the 'gold standard' in medical research for establishing the efficacy of medical interventions, including adverse reactions and side-effects. It was the logical outcome of the drive to put technological progress in the service of maximum efficiency and economy.

The statistically aggregated type replaces the anecdotal patient report of symptom as the basis for clinical diagnosis. As Trisha Greenhalgh puts it, in what has become the core text in the field of narrative medicine:

> In large research trials, the individual trial participant's unique and many-dimensioned experience is expressed as (say) a single dot on a scatter plot, to which we apply mathematical tools to produce a story about the sample as a whole. The *generalizable* truth that we seek to glean from research trials pertains to the sample's (and, it is hoped, the population's) story, not the individual trial participant's stories. The truths established by trials cannot be mechanistically applied to individual patients or episodes of illness whose behavior is irremediably contextual.[12]

For Greenhalgh, narrative is demanded as much epistemologically as humanistically. The mission of narrative-based medicine is not to reject the principles of clinical epidemiology or to demand an inversion of the hierarchy of evidence so that personal anecdote carries more weight in clinical decision-making than the Randomized Controlled Trial. Rather, the position is that, without the inclusion of the patient's subjective dimension, the reliance on objective explanation alone is unscientific. 'The valid application of empirical evidence *requires* a solid grounding in the narrative-based world'[13] [emphasis in original].

Nonetheless, being irreducible to a dot or statistic, while often not being susceptible to standardized treatments, the individual may be able to do no more than insecurely hold together the amorphous content of a complexly particular life. An authentically engaged understanding of that life and self might yield not answers but the terrifying lack of them, a sense of the profound ill-fittedness of this person's needs to what is possible for the doctor to prescribe.

For Arthur Frank, in his seminal text, *The Wounded Storyteller*, it is precisely because an individual's story might not fit into anything except itself, that the ill person needs to tell it every bit as much as the physician needs to hear it. Illness brings sudden change and often chaos, more or less, to the sufferer. Thus vulnerable as never before, patients within the hospital system accumulate entries on medical charts that become the official story of their illness and they can begin to think of themselves as no longer people, but as cases. The question 'How are you?' needs a context wider than the medical report if only to enable the patient personally to feel and to suffer the loss of habitual routines and separation from past experience. Health care requires recognition that this is still a personal life and not just one crippled by incurable or progressive illness.[14]

Substituting personal narrative for the conventional medical report is really like putting literature into medicine in a practical way. As Frank suggests, the difference between the standard case history and the patient's own story is very often this: the patient tells his or her story at the point when, with the onset of illness, the story of the person's life seems ended but the life itself carries on. At its best, personal biography occupies the same terrain as literary story; it is more a probing than a precision tool—a way of feeling out where a person is in life, and where he or she may be going. At the same time, the listening doctor, like the reader, must attend to what is individual, unique, particular. The 'narrative practitioner', says Rita Charon in *Narrative Medicine*, uses 'the narrative skills of recognizing, absorbing, interpreting and being moved by the plights of patients in all their complexity'.[15] When doctor and patient thus occupy, from different needs or perspectives, the place of the novelist, then what we call 'literary' in story has a real-life presence in medical practice.

At the same time, the sense of alienation an ill person suffers is not just the fault of the hospital or depersonalizing medical care. Illness brings with it a consciousness for the first time of not simply inhabiting, but of being, a body. In health, our attention is directed outwards, to life situations that are not about the body, where the body's perceptions tell of the world, not of itself. When, in illness, the body's functioning is no longer mere background, this is not just a reversal of priorities but a disturbance in the very structures of self-orientation. Carl Edvard Rudebeck cites the case of Rachel, diagnosed with diabetes at the age of ten. When the need to give herself injections is explained, she thinks: 'I will be digging holes every day in my own skin.' Suddenly the body is not the medium of her own life, but itself an existing thing. '*My own skin*' is a stunned recognition of herself as vulnerably physical. Moreover, the 'I', which only hours before was simply at home in the body, now exists in alienated and aggressive relation to it. The separation of the 'I' that 'digs' and the 'my' that feels it is a symptom of Rachel's being split between identification with the disease and its treatment, on the one hand, and her primary need for protection from it (her skin's biological *function*), on the other. The nature of her illness means that Rachel no longer feels whole in any sense.[16]

Yet Rachel's brokenness is still instinctively expressible here in the child. But in the adult it is often too hardened or too deep for ready access. Then, it is the very struggle for expression that is more palpable rather than a readily available personal story.

The classic text on the special role of the doctor in relation to people's buried lives is John Berger's *A Fortunate Man*, published in the 1960s. Combining visual image, essay and memoir, and thus pitched somewhere between the novel and photojournalism, it tells the real-life story of John Sassall, an English country doctor practising in an impoverished rural community. Early in the book, Berger recounts Dr Sassall's visit to a new patient, a woman in her late twenties, who has recently moved to the area with her husband and three children, and is squatting in an abandoned farmhouse in abject poverty, cold and squalor. The woman has been getting out of breath and, when she bends down to pick something up, she can barely stand up again. 'Doctor, can a woman of my age have heart trouble?' she asks. Examining her chest, Sassall promises she does not have a serious heart disease. Then he asks whether she and her husband intend to stay in the area and what they would think if he tried to get them better housing: 'You have to ask Jack about that. We do everything fifty-fifty':

'You can't go on like this. You know that don't you? We've got to get you out of here -'

'There's lots more unfortunate than us,' she said.

The doctor laughed, and then so did she. She was still young enough for her face to change totally with her expression. Her face looked capable of surprise again. [...]

'Where were you living before you came here?'

'In Cornwall. It was lovely there by the sea. Look.'

A photograph showed herself in high-heeled shoes, a tight skirt and a chiffon scarf round her head with a man and a small child walking along a beach.

'That's your husband?'

'No that's not Jack, that's Cliff and Stephen.'

The doctor nodded, surprised.

'I'll say that for Jack,' she continued, 'he never makes no distinction between the kids that are his and those that are mine like. We share fifty-fifty. He's better to Steve than his own father. It's just that he can't touch me.'[17]

It is not the stethoscope but the photograph that begins to uncover the true source of the woman's heart trouble and the real depth of her privation. The sudden presence of the woman's past releases a buried personal strata which, once touched off, swiftly dismantles her default marital attitude ('we do everything fifty-fifty'). It summons a more vulnerably expressive and personal mode in which scrupulous fairness is replaced by a confusing emotional mix of hurt at her husband's coldness, and honest appreciation of his worth as a father. All this happens at all, because the doctor risks breaching the woman's stoic defences—' "There's lots more unfortunate than us" ...The doctor laughed, and then so did she.' Her instinctive response is what first encourages him to ask the question which invites personal story—'Where were you living before?' The photograph now renews *his own* capacity for surprise at *her* hidden potential—not for change of demeanour merely, but for a wholly different form of life. Here is one of those essential but unpredictable ingredients of what Balint calls 'atmosphere', a mutual openness to the live promptings of the moment.

> She looked at the photograph holding it out at arm's length.
> Still holding the photograph, she let her arm fall on to her lap,
> and looked at the doctor, her eyes now angry.

'It just doesn't mean anything to me. It doesn't touch me.
I know what real love is like, you see. With the father of Stephen,
when I got Stephen, it was beautiful. I know what they mean
when they say it is the most wonderful thing in the world, it was
like that when I got Stephen and he wanted me like that. And
I shall never forget it – I lie awake and think of it yet – because
it has never been like that again when it was like heaven when
I got Stephen.'[18]

This woman does not simply 'tell the story' behind the photograph;
rather, this is a triggered happening, closer in form to Thomas
Hardy's poem 'The Photograph': 'Then I vented a cry of hurt, and
averted my eyes;/The spectacle was one that I could not bear,/To
my deep and sad surprise'. It is as though for the first time, in that
long silent gaze upon her lost life, she begins to allow into consciousness some true measure of what its loss really means. Personal
story is here a form for thinking into experience which does not
permit of simple or straightforward telling. For the memory of
what was 'beautiful' includes conventional sexual fulfilment, of
course. But it also involves a knowledge of 'real love' wherein, in
recollection of this 'heaven', not only her husband (Jack) but also
her lover (Cliff) are displaced by her son (Stephen), to whom they
are both now 'father'. This is not consolation so much as some deep
primal knot. Only the woman's hesitant articulation, drawn from
the profound capacity angrily to suffer her frustration as much as to
feel her deep love, can justly gather or order these elemental matters. 'It has never been like that again' is a terrible summation. But
it is also new-sprung realization. In this, more than all, she shows
herself 'capable of surprise again'. Precisely in not being formally
literary, this ordinary person's story helps show what literary thinking itself is really for: recognizing and refining what humans need,
even what they can sometimes do in life itself, by way of expression
and search.

'The doctor's business', says Dowrick emphatically, is not only to
listen to the ill person's story, but 'to help the patient find some
meaning and purpose out of seemingly undifferentiated suffering
and distress'.[19] When medicine thus stretches to include within itself
what is not open to definite cure, then it is indeed more art than

science. Rita Charon quotes the American twentieth-century literary critic, R. W. B. Lewis:

> 'Narrative deals with experiences, not with propositions.' Unlike scientific or epidemiological knowledge, which tries to discover things about the natural word that are universally true, narrative knowledge enables one individual to understand particular events befalling another individual not as an instance of something that is universally true but as a singular and meaningful situation.[20]

It is not that scientific understanding is simply forgotten in narrative medicine. Rather, narrative practice enables background general principles and expertise to be *sunk back into* singular cases.

It is no coincidence that doctors such as Iona Heath and Chris Dowrick, and those in the narrative medicine movement generally, should look to the arts, and to literature in particular, as an indispensable guide for their work. Like general practice itself at its most concerned, says Iona Heath, great literature 'is grounded in the intransigence of nature and the contingency of experience and allows no room to good intentions and wishful thinking'.[21] It is not simply that these doctors learn from literary works or re-apply to their own practice narrative techniques they find within them. It is rather as though they are already analogous to novelists—novelists of practical life—inhabiting the same intractable areas and using what is sometimes over-narrowly thought of as literary thinking in non-literary settings.

What is crucial is to understand what literary thinking is, whether in literature or life, what help it offers, and how it is best understood and practised.

Against Narrative?

In their conclusion to the opening chapter of *Narrative-Based Medicine*, Trisha Greenhalgh and Brian Hurwitz warmly acknowledge the crucial founding influence of the Balint tradition: its recognition that illness is embodied in a particular, unique individual; that subjective experience of illness is not mere data for medical propositions; that personal suffering needs acknowledgement, elicitation, and witness.

Yet they also lament that this legacy 'has not, for the most part, led to measurable changes in the way medicine is practised or accredited, and has not given rise to a significant programme of systematic research into the analysis and therapeutic use of narrative in the consultation'.[22]

As my previous section suggested, *Narrative-Based Medicine* explicitly offers itself as 'redressing that deficit' and laying the foundation for the legitimization and systemization of the practice as an alternative, and not merely secondary, model of medical care. It is a key step in the establishment of narrative-based medicine as a recognized discipline.

Yet my own concern in this section is what might also be lost from the successful institutionalization of narrative medicine's mission. What has happened, I wish to ask, to the idea of 'narrative' as it has undergone semi-incorporation into mainstream academic and clinical medicine? Everyone agrees—perhaps too readily—how important is story as the key expressive form for human accounts. But what does narrative as an entity or process mean to health practitioners and what does it do for their patients?

Establishing the practice of narrative medicine has faced two key and related challenges. First, the difficulty of embedding a person-centred practice within a medical culture to which it exists in resistant opposition. Medical students who respond warmly to richly diverse and nuanced doctor and patient stories in training, are no less vulnerable, in busily demanding hospital practice, to the power of a general unifying medical language which offers to patients a homogeneously rationalized and medicalized experience in place of their own.[23] Second, there is the issue of conferring upon narrative medicine the status of a formal discipline with its own general principles. Such theoretical robustness offers protection against the characterization of narrative medicine as a species of allegedly 'soft' (bad) as opposed to 'hard' (good) medical science. This is the same sort of strong theoretical defence that literary studies itself has sought in order to avoid the ever-lingering charges of liberal humanism and belles-lettres subjectivism. Indeed, narrative medicine has made use of theories of narrative in literature, as well as in philosophy, anthropology, and social science, to give academic gravitas and grounding to itself as a discipline rather than a vague or ill-defined 'approach'. But a practice that emerged, and which by definition operates amid the particularities of both situation and relationship, and which, as we have seen, is committed to rescuing or attending to the 'not-fitting' in human experience, is itself inimical to rigid conceptual frames.

Let me return, by way of illustration of this latter point, to the very sources of the narrative movement: Balint's research with GPs. His salient findings, in respect of how to arrive at a 'different, deeper, more comprehensive' understanding of the patient's suffering, began with the recognition that 'structuring the doctor–patient relationship on the pattern of a physical examination inactivates the processes the doctor wants to observe'.[24]

The doctor must work, therefore, from a different place. Balint's guidance in this matter is presented in two successive chapters. 'How to Start', from which I quoted earlier, demonstrates the crucial importance of 'listening', as distinct from the traditional medical history-taking. The instruction that the doctor must *learn to listen* and learn by *doing* it, is an austere one, the first rule in demanding a more exacting form of diagnosis. In 'When to Stop', 'the important factor,' says Balint, 'is difficult to describe':

> Perhaps it might be called a sense of proportion. A 'long interview' is a give-and-take affair. The patient gives a great deal to his doctor, his confidence, some jealously guarded secrets, which may sometimes appear insignificant or even puerile to an outsider, but mean a great deal to him. If not enough happens to restore the balance, the patient is bound to feel despoiled, robbed or cheated.... It is exceedingly difficult to state exactly what it is that restores the balance, so that after the 'long interview' the patient feels understood, relieved, or even enriched, instead of being despoiled or cheated. The difference is not what is called 'correct interpretation' though correct interpretation forms a part of it. Neither is it 'reassurance'... Perhaps the best that I can offer is to say that an experienced doctor has some idea 'when to stop'.[25]

As a taxonomy of 'How to's' these are wonderfully *in*definite precepts: 'difficult to describe', 'exceedingly difficult to state exactly' 'the difference is not what is called "correct interpretation"', but, says Balint, it is not *not* that either. The only certainty, as we saw in 'How to Start', is the out-of-place-ness of the certainties of medical knowledge itself. 'Our experience has invariably been that, *if the doctor asks questions in the manner of medical history-taking, he will always get answers – but hardly anything more.*' To 'listen' is not just the first but the only rule. Every other procedural propriety must take its cue, colour and tone from this attentiveness to the particularity of the relationship and the present moment of disclosure itself. This is the art of the implicit and the tacit. Upon the doctor's having this talent or not, more or less, depends the surrounding atmosphere. The doctor partly brings this with him or her, as personal influence, and for that reason alone, atmosphere, 'far from being standardized', is always—for better or worse— irreducibly itself, uncategorizable and unique. But this special atmosphere can also be something created, in the moment:

> While discovering in himself an ability to listen to things in his patient that are barely spoken because the patient himself is only dimly aware of them, the doctor will start listening to the same kind of language in himself'.[26]

'To listen to things in his patient'; 'things' is wonderfully indefinite here, a sign of attunement to the nebulous content of the patient's experience, to the 'meaning' inside what externally 'might appear insignificant or even puerile'. But listening to the patient out there is simultaneously a listening in here, a delicate and involuntary instrument for finding the hidden content, the very language, from within the doctor's own inner self. What Balint calls 'atmosphere' is something like a third presence, or listened-for voice, that is called into being for both persons together.

What demonstrably lies behind the narrative medicine movement is a will to create precisely the non-bureaucratized, non-standardized, non-institutionalized spaces for events of human expressiveness or truth—'beingness' as an early disciple of Balint's put it—which Balint's research witnesses and advocates. To this day, Balint's practice-based research remains an indispensable model for practitioners and teachers in this field.[27]

Yet what has been taken from Balint's work is his emphasis not on the creation of 'atmosphere' but on the giving of case history, when Balint himself never uses the terms 'narrative' or 'story'. In part, this exclusive concentration on story has been deliberate, as John Launer

explains in his account of the relation of narrative approaches to the
Balint tradition in *Narrative-Based Primary Care*. Narrative in medical
practice has wanted to resist the 'paternalistic' assumptions and inva-
sive questioning and procedures used in psychoanalytic approaches
to care. It has also sought to broaden the contexts for understanding
patient health, looking beyond the psychological to include, for
example, the social and environmental conditions in which a person
lives. Narrative-based medicine has thus defined itself almost equally
against its closer partner, psychoanalysis, as against its greatest antag-
onist, Evidence-Based Medicine, which seeks to derive generalizable
scientific laws from the statistical analysis of vast samples of imper-
sonal data. Narrative occupies a middle ground between the 'expert'
interpretation associated with both camps, and, Launer argues, offers
a form of understanding and a language democratically available
to all.[28]

What this process of embedding narrative in medicine means,
however, is that Balint's key instruments for finding the patient's personal reality—'listening' and, especially 'atmosphere'—have become
conceptually (if not always actually and practically) subordinated to
an emphasis on narrative as the chief elicitation tool. The effect of
substituting for Balint's mode of attentive listening the autonomy of
the storyteller runs the risk of denying to the patient, I will argue,
what he or she is really in search of, and most needs.

Here, for instance, is a Balint case history where the doctors in the
study agree that it would be wholly a mistake simply to accept the
patient's own account. For this story is so 'set' as to be of a different
species to the encouraged personal narrative messily arising on the
spot out of proper doctorly help.

Miss F, a twenty-four-year-old secretary, the only child of an upper-
middle-class family, had been ill for almost a decade, since an attack
of food poisoning which affected several girls, all of whom, apart from
Miss F, returned to normal school life after a few days. She gave this
account of the history of her condition on application for the psychiatric treatment to which she was referred by her GP.

> When I was fifteen at boarding school I had food poisoning, but
> only fairly slightly. I became very thin indeed and worried
> myself a good deal because I worried I should get behind my

form in work. In fact I had a nervous breakdown and my hair fell out badly. I stayed at home for a year and gradually put on weight, returning to a smaller boarding school when I was much fitter. It was at this school that I began to notice my legs swelling and they became gradually worse over a period of time until my doctor prescribed Mersalyl [mercury] injections but these only slimmed my legs temporarily. Since that time I have had numerous injections also to get my monthly period going again (which completely disappeared after the food-poisoning when I was fifteen). About a year or eighteen months ago I started a very nasty irritable rash. The skin specialist diagnosed this as due to nervous tension. This will not go altogether and seems to come in spasms especially if I am going to a party and want to be clear. I find it very difficult to relax and I work myself up very much when going to a party or anything. I find I lack confidence. I broke off an engagement nine months ago as I felt my fiancé was losing interest in me. This upset me a great deal and my rash increased, and also the swelling of my legs. I felt it was due to my legs and the unsightly rash that I lost my boyfriend.[29]

For Balint, profound personal reality, in Miss F's case, is occluded by the patient's more limited and superficial accounting of what is wrong. She has not only told this story before; the more she tells it the closer it comes to a clinical re-telling. The tendency of her whole account is always for the visible physical *symptoms*—the rash, the swelling—to be turned back into *cause*: 'I felt it was due to my legs and the unsightly rash that I lost my boyfriend'. The whole narrative veers unevenly between physical and psychosomatic explanations, between temporally definite and invisibly 'nervous' origins. Thus, underlying causes do not emerge from within herself with the certainty of personal discovery; rather cause and effect are improvised from within the story sequence.

Yet this account is incoherent just because it is a narrative seeking coherence or tangible explanations—*this* causes *that*—which it cannot stably find and cannot cease looking for. One senses this version of Miss F's story could carry unstoppably on and on in its knock-on sequence—I am ill, ugly, and undesirable, this makes me worry and makes me worse, but the cause is really organic and I need medicine to cure it—until it turns into and actually constitutes her life story. This is in fact what happened. After four psychiatric treatments, Miss F reverted to long-term use of injections and drugs and collecting doctors.

For Balint, it is not only that 'depth' always takes absolute priority over the linear dimension of story. It is a depth of being of which the patient himself or herself may be 'only dimly aware', and by definition unable to translate into straightforward causal narrative. Story, that is to say, is not the *necessary*, and may not be the *available* form.

Indeed, as Miss F's case shows, albeit in a narrative still inflected with the rigidities of a standard medical view, autobiographical story may be the *wrong* mode. Intrinsically, if inadvertently, that is to say, the stories we tend to tell of ourselves are liable to *betray* deep-lying personal truth. So Galen Strawson argues, in 'Against Narrativity', where he takes issue with the widespread advocacy of self-storying as a radically reconstitutive and enabling practice, and attacks its potentially disaunthenticating or distorting relation to human experience. Narrative's most pernicious tendency, he says, is precisely to falsify self and experience:

Telling and retelling one's past leads to changes, smoothings, enhancements, shifts away from the facts, and recent research has shown that this is not just a human psychological foible. It turns out to be an inevitable consequence of the mechanics of the neurophysiological process of laying down memories that every studied conscious recall of past events brings an alteration. The implication is plain: the more you recall, retell, narrate yourself, the further you risk moving away from accurate self-understanding, from the truth of your being. Some are constantly telling their daily experiences to others in a storying way and with great gusto. They are drifting ever further off the truth.[30]

The tendency to look for story or narrative coherence in one's life is ironically, he argues, 'a gross hindrance to self-understanding; to a just, general, practically real sense, implicit or explicit, of one's nature'. Because it is a fact of human psychology that conscious recall of past events brings alteration, one is almost certain to get one's 'story' wrong, to create only another stereotype in place of a medical one. The problem of studied articulation and over-conscious knowing of one's story might well be intensified in medical settings where the telling of patient stories is officially sanctioned.

Moreover, the very capacity for narrative form to substitute for content might be damaging, for masquerading, in Hannah Arendt's phrase, as 'mastery' of experience. 'Narration of the past,' she wrote, 'solves no problems and assuages no suffering: it does not master anything once and for all. Rather, as long as the meaning of the events remains alive . . . mastering of the past can take the form of ever recurrent narration'.[31] All too often, stories become for the most of us who are not novelists a formulaic or conventional account which in its very extendedness overtakes its own teller, producing a normalized and overly consistent coherence inappropriate to a creature incapable (for better and worse) of *wholly* knowing the shape or purpose of its own life.

So tepid or predictable a version of personal story is a far cry of course from the depth and richness that narrative medicine is actually seeking, and for which literary narrative is always its prior model. Both Rita Charon in *Narrative Medicine*, and Trisha Greenhalgh and Brian Hurwitz in *Narrative-Based Medicine* find a defining touchstone for the theoretical framing of narrative medicine in the important distinction made by the early twentieth-century pioneer in the field of literary reading and teaching, Louise Rosenblatt. 'Literature,' she said 'provides *living through* not simply *knowledge about*'.[32] This then, as we have seen, is what narrative medicine essentially borrows from the literary field: a keen valuing of a language which encompasses and transmits the lived experience of individual being in opposition to the 'knowledge about' mode exclusively prioritized by biomedical science. 'Narrative offers a possibility of *understanding,*' as Greenhalgh and Hurwitz put it, 'which cannot be arrived at by any other means'.[33]

But what is most worrying for me in this present book is that narrative medicine seems not to recognize or acknowledge the difference between the deep-textured understanding offered by what Rosenblatt calls 'the literary experience' (p. 24) and the more simple and direct one produced by confessional autobiography. Narrative medicine, in other words, does not always sufficiently discriminate between the simple *literal* and the more multi-layered *literary* story. Instead, an impoverished and over-simplified definition of narrative comes to stand for all. According to Rita Charon:

> When we try to understand why things happen we put events in temporal order, making decisions about beginnings, middles and ends or causes and effects by virtue of imposing plots on otherwise chaotic events.... By telling stories to ourselves and others – in dreams, in diaries, in friendships, in marriages, in therapy sessions – we grow slowly not only to know who we are but also to become who we are.[34]

But these 'decisions' are indeed impositions. 'Narrative' undergoes precisely the processes of standardization here that its incorporation in medical practice is designed to modify. Storytelling, as illustrated and defined here, does not belong to the literary at all, except reductively. More, in making 'story' an imposed fiction, this does wrong to life as well as to literature. We know from Bion that deeply personal experience—the reality of 'who we are'—is not susceptible to facile 'knowing' or tidy expression, other than distortingly. There is always, Bion says, an available terminology to be found in material that is superficial and easily accessible to consciousness. The problem of finding the right word, he goes on, 'is analogous to that of the sculptor finding his form in the block of his material, of the musician finding the formula of musical notation within the sounds he hears, of the man of action finding the actions that represent his thoughts'.[35] Form is not applied but found; authentic story reveals the form hidden within experience. It is hard, struggling work; it is, Bion suggests, one of the most profoundly creative acts of being alive.

Indeed, for Balint himself, the founder of story in medicine, the kind of 'putting in order' which defines Charon's idea of story comes far too easily to be commensurate with actual experience. 'The mind is multi-dimensional to an impossible degree whereas any description is limited to one dimension':

> Language can describe only one sequence of events at a time; if several occur simultaneously, language has to jump to and fro among the parallel lines, creating difficulties, if not confusion, for the listener. A further, almost insurmountable complication is caused by the fact that mental events not only take place

simultaneously along parallel lines, but influence each other profoundly.[36]

Neurologists tell us that we are programmed to tell stories, and that the will to 'impose' order on chaos is part of our biological hard-wiring.[37] But then our creaturely disposition, at brain level, is apparently at odds with our mind's experience of what happens to us. Experience possesses a complex simultaneity and multiplicity which is of a wholly different order from the linearity and singularity of conventional ideas of story.

The danger of the single story, says novelist Chimamanda Adichie, is that it *creates* stereotypes as much as it conforms to them. Born into a conventional middle-class family in Nigeria, Adichie had always felt pity for the family's live-in house-boy because all she had ever been told about him was that his family was very poor:

> One Saturday we went to his village to visit, and his mother showed us a beautifully patterned basket made of dyed raffia that his brother had made. I was startled. It had not occurred to me that anybody in his family could actually make something. It had become impossible for me to see them as anything but poor. Their poverty was my single story of them.

The problem with the stereotyping single story, Adichie concludes, is not that they are untrue, but that they are incomplete. 'They make one story become the only story.'[38]

Adichie's account is an explanation of why she became a novelist. For in literary narrative the possibility is always open for the formal default or definitive story to give way to the complex and overlapping realities that is the real form of experience.

So, in order to demonstrate what literary narrative actually is and does, I choose a work that seems to me the fairest test case in this context. *Janet's Repentance* is the final novella in *Scenes of Clerical Life*, the first published fiction of the nineteenth-century pioneer of literary realism, George Eliot. This is the work where George Eliot first showed she had learnt her craft as a realist. It tells the story of Janet Dempster, a desperately unhappy wife, who, long the victim of her brute drunken husband's violence, and, childless and often alone, has herself been driven to the consolation of drink and is now an alcoholic. One scientist has claimed that George Eliot's portrayal of Janet Dempster gives a far more accurate depiction of Type 1 alcoholism, associated with high 'reward dependency' and 'harm avoidance', than does the typology given in the Diagnostic and Statistical Manual of Mental Health Disorders (DSM), from which these categories derive.[39] This unflinching accuracy in relation to a stigmatized issue (especially in the nineteenth century and especially in a middle-class woman) is a measure of how, even explicitly, this novella is defiant of standardized norms and, as George Eliot herself puts it, of those 'facile' generalizations which 'prejudge individuals by means of formulae, and cast them...into duly lettered pigeon holes' (*Janet's Repentance*, Chapter Eight). Indeed, this fiction rests on precisely the belief that underwrites narrative medicine at its finest: 'The only true knowledge of our fellow-man is that which enables us to *feel with* him...the life and death struggles of separate human being' (*Janet's Repentance*, Chapter Eleven, my emphasis). George Eliot made one of her greatest realist creations out of what otherwise would have been mere stereotype.

The climax of Janet's story is the moment when she defies her husband, almost daring him to kill her. Instead, in the dead of a bitter winter's night, Janet is 'thrust out from her husband's home in her thin night-dress, the harsh wind cutting her naked feet':

> When Janet sat down shivering on the door-stone, with the door shut upon her past life, and the future black and unshapen before her as the night, the scenes of her childhood, her youth and her painful womanhood, rushed back upon her consciousness, and made one picture with her present desolation. The petted child taking her newest toy to bed with her—the young girl, proud in strength and beauty, dreaming that life was an easy thing, and that it was pitiful weakness to be unhappy—the bride, passing with trembling joy from the outer court to the inner sanctuary of woman's life—the wife, beginning her initiation into sorrow, wounded, resenting, yet still hoping and forgiving—the poor bruised woman, seeking through weary years the one refuge of despair, oblivion:—Janet seemed to herself all these in the same moment that she was conscious of being seated on the cold stone under the shock of a new misery. (Chapter Fifteen)

'We are condemned', says Raymond Tallis, 'to live in a world made up of tiny moments, linked by And Then, And Then.'[40] But here, just for a moment, Janet's life is released from apparently arbitrary consecutive extension to make, agonizingly, 'one picture'. Child, girl, bride, wife, woman have simultaneous, and all too painfully connected, reality. For a space, Janet is in complete possession, temporarily, of everything her unfulfilled life is not, will never be, and yet still might have been. This is the deepest human reality of all—when experience is no longer containable within habitual ordinary categories, and none of the normal rules applies. How could these all be part of the same narrative? All this time the narrative remains bound to the limiting framework of common language and ordinary event. Janet is still seated on the cold door-stone, an unhappy wife, in a small provincial town. But she inhabits a reality both tied to and 'more than' the mundane human material out of which it emerges.

So, when Janet awaits the coming of daybreak:

> The future took shape after shape of misery before her, always ending in her being dragged back again to her old life of terror, and stupor, and fevered despair. Her husband had so long overshadowed her life that her imagination could not keep hold of a condition in which that great dread was absent; and even his absence—what was it? only a dreary vacant flat, where there was nothing to strive after, nothing to long for.
> (Chapter Sixteen)

Janet has left a bad story—her abusive husband and unhappy marriage. Better if she had walked out herself, of course, but even this way there is a chance for a new life away from her husband. But this does not feel like a second chance. Instead Janet finds she cannot get out of her own story of internalized punishment and pain. Even now, as day is literally following night, Janet must be 'dragged back again', the only future 'before her' an unending repetition of her past self and life. It feels as though she will turn to drink again, all the more certainly now to replace or evade the very absence of the dread which had driven her to drink in the first place.

The novella's imaginative duty is to the inner aftermath which cannot fit into a straightforward narrative of escape or loss. It is an experience that (like Ian's sense of 'no point' in Chris Dowrick's case history) might otherwise be lost to subterranean inwardness, and for which there so often is no external voice or witness in ordinary life. 'No eye rested on Janet as she sank down on the cold stone, and looked into the dismal night.... Oh, if some ray of hope, of pity, of consolation, would pierce through the horrible gloom.' This is what the literary imagination is for in George Eliot's work: to find the intimately personal story that is occluded by the gross and definite one.

It is no easier when Janet's husband is now dead, and she seems fully embarked on a new life. She is still fighting her addiction and vulnerable to discouragement and fear at the mere prospect of returning home to the 'vacant dining room'. When she inadvertently discovers a decanter of the dead Dempster's brandy hidden in a drawer, desire overwhelms her, and she dashes it to the ground and flees:

> Where should she go? In what place would this demon that had re-entered her be scared back again?... Now, when the paroxysm of temptation was past, dread and despondency began to thrust themselves, like cold heavy mists... The temptation would come again – that rush of desire might master her the next time – she would slip back again into that deep slimy pit from which she had once been rescued, and there might be no deliverance for her more. (Chapter Twenty-five)

Again, it is when the crisis is ostensibly past, when the temptation is over and actually conquered, in the interstices of conventional story, that Janet feels at her most powerless. Janet's real needs are as undefined as that 'vacancy' which frightens her so. Yet she is so full of those needs that she has no sense of how well she has done in not giving in to them—in smashing that bottle instead of drinking it. She feels only the fear of temptation and nothing at all of her great achievement in resisting it. Think of the story a real-life Janet would tell of her own life. It could only be a victim's: I am an alcoholic, an abused wife, a failure. I am always afraid I will drink again. Only the novel, by subvocally capturing the deeper reality of hidden struggle, with its agonies *and* its brave resistances, can find in Janet's story something other than defeat.

This prose might be regarded, I say, as the original prototype of narrative medicine, hearing the suffering of human creatures, capturing what lies behind the bald narrative facts of all too ordinary and common alcoholism, abuse, and depression. The scientist who admired the portrayal of Janet ventured that were George Eliot alive today she might well have been a doctor, so intense is the humanity of her understanding of human suffering.

But as a novelist, not a doctor, George Eliot had her own delicate instrument for finding, as Balint with his patients, her creatures' secret inner lives. In formal terms, these passages offer instances of free indirect discourse—that mode of narration which belongs neither internally to character, nor externally to narrator, but exists between the two: It isn't 'Where should I go?' but 'Where should she go...The temptation would come again'; 'What was [her husband's absence]?, only a dreary vacant flat, where there was nothing to strive after, nothing to long for'. Free indirect discourse tells the experience of a person's life, as he or she never quite lives it.[41] For neither free indirect discourse, nor the so-called omniscience of author-narrator, are of course truly 'there' for Janet herself in any sense. The character does not know of an author; she cannot see or hear her own thoughts as the reader does. This is not fictive naivety or simplistic realist convention. It is a belief in what is there even when—especially when—humans cannot realize it as characters in life.

In this novel, free indirect discourse takes the place of the ancient religious practice of confession—occurring in the novel at just those crises when Janet's literal confessor, the minister Tryan, is absent. At once a descendant and a secular replacement for religious discourse, free indirect mode was to become the realist novel's most sophisticated tool for emotional attunement, for listening in to its creatures, hearing thoughts that are often inadmissible or unavailable to the individuals who most need to have or hear them. For we do not have access to, we can barely hold, all that we contain. This is not a deficiency, but one of the rules.

One thing that Janet does not know is that her second story has already begun, much earlier and more quietly. This is when she first encounters Tryan, the Evangelical minister, whose teachings she and her husband had opposed through party interests. She overhears him comforting a dying parishioner.

> Janet was surprised; the tone and the words were so unlike what she had expected to hear. Mr Tryan had his deeply-felt troubles,

then, like herself?...The softening thought was in her eyes
when he appeared in the doorway, pale, weary, and depressed.
The sight of Janet standing there with the entire absence of
self-consciousness which belongs to a new and vivid impression,
made him start and pause a little. Their eyes met, and they
looked at each other gravely for a few moments. Then they
bowed, and Mr Tryan passed out. (Chapter Twelve)

Her surprise at his depth of feeling begets his own startled sense of
something newly serious in her. For the instant they can see one
another truly, because, thus momentarily, they are 'unlike' themselves.
It is a happening so passing and slight as hardly to qualify as an event
at all. Yet, at a moment of deepest trial, the recollection of this fleeting
instant alone has power to save Janet:

She suddenly thought—and the thought was like an electric
shock—there was one spot in her memory which seemed to
promise her as an untried spring, where the waters might
be sweet. That short interview with Mr Tryan had come
back upon her—his voice, his words, his look. (Chapter
Sixteen)

The tiniest emotional shocks not only reverberate through time but
have power virtually to create a new life. This is something within
personal narrative that is not just narrative or a conventional view of
a known opponent—something closer to the lyric intensity and emotional fulfilment of poetry. The moment of initiation really constitutes
consummation, though neither Janet nor Tryan can know it. For this
is a love story which, non-stereotypically, is unable to fulfil itself in
time. Even at the point of Tryan's death, 'the time was *not yet* come for
Janet to be conscious that the hold he had on her heart was any other
than that of the heaven-sent friend' (Chapter Twenty-seven).

   Literary prose registers not only the prosaic reality but the poetry
that exists hiddenly and precariously within the prose of life. 'Depend
upon it,' says George Eliot, in the first story of *Scenes of Clerical Life*,
'you would gain unspeakably if you would learn with me to see some
of the poetry and the pathos, the tragedy and the comedy, lying in
the experience of a human soul that looks out through dull grey eyes,
and that speaks in a voice of quite ordinary tones' ('Amos Barton',

Chapter Five). This is how narrative implicitly gives notice that poetry, rather than narrative, is in some version of itself the highest and best index of how humans are always bigger and more complex than the story they inhabit.

****

It is to poetry, then, that I now turn in order to demonstrate that the lyric mode is at least as essential as narrative in releasing experience from the bondage of inarticulacy or conventionalism. In what follows, the poet, Elizabeth Barrett Browning, is not an author separate from a character in her story, but herself writing from within the thick of experience.

Elizabeth Barrett's relationship with Robert Browning exists in the popular imagination and often in biographical accounts as a sudden drama of happiness and a great love story. Elizabeth Barrett suffered long years of invalidism and of seclusion, in which she was subject to the idiosyncratic obsessions of a neurotic-possessive father, and, latterly, to grief and guilt over the death of her younger brother. Then, at the age of forty, following a two-year secret courtship, she left home and family for a life with Browning in Italy where, as wife, mother and poet, she flourished until her death.

The intimate autobiographical records, however, uncover what really lay behind these bald contours, long conventionalized as narrative in Rudolph Besier's sentimental play-made-film *The Barretts of Wimpole Street*. The famous correspondence between the couple show this love story to have been a slow, painful, almost involuntary and vulnerable journey, full of resistances and refusals to the change that love both offered and seemed to demand. When Browning first declared his love for her, Elizabeth Barrett 'recoiled by instinct and at the first glance, yet conclusively'. His 'wild speakings', she wrote to him, must 'die out between *you and me alone*, like a misprint between you and the printer.' '*I must not*...I *will not see you again* – and you will justify me later in your heart.' She was as moved by the power of his love as she was fearful of its capacity to last. 'It affects me and has affected me, very deeply, that you should persist *so* – and sometimes I have felt you might mistake, a little unconsciously, the strength of your own feeling'. Though doubtful of it, she could believe in his love for her far more readily than she could believe herself to be worthy of it:

What could I speak that would not be unjust to you? Your life! if you gave it to me and I put my whole heart into it; what should I put but anxiety, and more sadness than you were born to? What could I give you, which it would not be ungenerous to give?

Neither love given, nor love received, could be counted by Elizabeth Barrett as a simple and certain good. For, above all, love was not the ecstatic fulfilment of a conventional single person's narrative, but the bewilderment of having believed yourself to be in one quite definite story, only suddenly to find yourself in another. 'I had done living, I thought,' she told Browning, 'when you came and sought me out.' 'My life was *ended* when I knew you, and if I survive myself it is for your sake.' Thus to live or begin again in a different form and order seemed more a kind of reckless and frightening temptation than rapturous release:

> Shall I tell you? it seems to me, to myself, that no man was ever before to any woman what you are to me - the fulness must be in proportion, you know, to the vacancy...and only *I* know what was behind - the long wilderness *without* the blossoming rose...and the capacity for happiness, like a black gaping hole, before this silver flooding. Is it wonderful that I should stand as in a dream, and disbelieve — not *you* - but my own fate? Was ever any one taken suddenly from a lampless dungeon and placed upon the pinnacle of a mountain, without the head turning round and the heart turning faint, as mine do?

The correspondence seems to say all that could be said in terms of honest written expression of love.[42]

Yet even while Elizabeth Barrett was personally confessing her love in almost daily correspondence, she was also secretly writing the love-sonnet sequence which was to become *Sonnets from the Portuguese*. The sonnets were never intended for publication and were not read by Browning himself until several years after their composition. Yet, like the letters which they were composed alongside, they are intimately addressed to Robert throughout. Why did Elizabeth Barrett do this? Why, that is to say, did she feel the need to say in poetry what she was already saying in recognizably similar language and in 'live' form in the letters?

The answer lies within the poems themselves. At the close of a sonnet from very early in the sequence, Elizabeth Barrett rehearses her peremptory rejection of Browning's first declaration of love: 'Stand farther off then. Go!' In the letters, she had meant to cancel once and for all the 'misprint' of his commitment to her. Yet here she reprises the refusal at the very opening of the subsequent sonnet, as though making space, in print, for all that is *not* concluded within herself.

> Yet I feel that I shall stand
> Henceforward in thy shadow. Nevermore
> Alone upon the threshold of my door
> Of individual life, I shall command
> The uses of my soul, nor lift my hand
> Serenely in the sunshine as before (Sonnet 6)

'Yet' emerges in sudden surprise that even separation now won't be complete. This does not feel to her like a story too good to be true but closer to a story she may not want. 'Nevermore/Alone'. In the merest turn from one line to another, the threshold and transition from one story to another is thus sharply and visibly crossed, and the feeling is as much one of loss and uncertainty as of gain: loss of singlehood, of lonely individuality, of one's very own life. It might not be much of a life but it is mine, this sonnet seems to say. How do I know this new one will be better?

This is why the letters were not enough. Robert Browning's love had given Elizabeth Barrett the promise of an unlooked-for second life. Without self-belief enough as yet to support its own self-emergence, the poetry offered a form in which this coming-to-life self could reside and do its consolidated thinking ahead of its full and secure realization in her. Poetry is here a preparation in transition for becoming the narrator of her own story. It gave a structure for expressive being not just in relation to Browning but for herself in the midst of change. This is not a provisional self but one fully present and alive in the strange place of movement and change *between* the old self of the lampless dungeons and the love fulfilment of the mountain top.

The resonant spaces of these sonnets make room for the delicate interstices and minute transition points for which conventional story has no time or form. The poems, to use Elizabeth Barrett's own expression, are 'a place to stand and love in for a day' (Sonnet 22),

protected from time and the hour even in going along with it. In this
sense of created 'place', these poems are paradigmatic of what
Balint really means by 'atmosphere'. They make possible a way of
thinking and a place for thinking that the world would certainly dis-
courage and for which it would have no appropriate tone. Where
else might a middle-aged woman in love for the first time securely
express her fears at the unprecedented change love has wrought in
the mode that is emotionally most fitting—the fragile tones and language of a child?:

> If I leave all for *thee,* wilt thou exchange
> And *be* all to me? Shall I never miss
> Home-talk and blessing and the common kiss
> That comes to each in turn, nor count it strange,
> When I look up, to drop on a new range
> Of walls and floors, . . . another home than this? (Sonnet 35)

Where else would these vulnerably childlike misgivings simultaneously discover the deep test and terms of grown-up love? It is an
exchange not merely of feeling, but of child for adult self, common for
exclusive kiss; *all* for *all*.

Above all, the poem is a protective casing and stimulus for the tactful emergence of the woman who fits neither the world's nor her own
prior forms: 'Yes call me by my pet-name,' she says in a late sonnet
and immediately regrets that she cannot answer with 'the same heart'
as when a child.

> Yet still my heart goes to thee . . . ponder how . . .
> Not as to a single good, but all my good!
> Lay thy hand on it, best one, allow
> That no child's foot could run as fast as this blood. (Sonnet 34)

In the thought spaces and in the very pulse of the poem, 'my heart'
finds, suddenly and acceptingly, an essential vitality that is neither child's,
nor old maid's. This is how this sequence discovers for Elizabeth
Barrett a new story in between the old one of dutiful daughter or
loveless spinster.

For when the sequence begins, this love story is not yet a narrative.
That is why it is written wholly in the present, rather than as
retrospective summary. What these sonnets really record and make
possible is the coming, in the midst of uncertainty, of a sudden burst

of recognition which says: 'This is what I am now. This is what is really happening'.

> And when I say at need
> *I love thee* .. mark! .. *I love thee!* .. in thy sight
> I stand transfigured, glorified aright,
> With conscience of the new rays that proceed
> Out of my face toward thine. (Sonnet 10)

The tiny gaps are an involuntary signal of surprise at overhearing her own words ('*I love thee*..'), as if writing them down unexpectedly makes them true to her as no 'misprint'. Then comes the accepting embodiment of those words—'mark! .. *I love thee* ..'—a commitment to a self that *can* live out the narrative those words initiate and imply. In the space between the first and second pronouncement, it is as if the words are finding power to *be* as well as to *feel*, that flash of transformation she describes in the final lines of this sonnet:

> And what I *feel*, across the inferior features
> Of what I *am*, doth flash itself, and show
> How that great work of Love enhances Nature's. (12–14)

Elizabeth Barrett had felt she was an unlovable woman, but love now made her beautiful—not just conventionally, out of the love that he gave her, but rather out of the love she felt for him, transforming the very features of her face.

It is no wonder that Elizabeth Barrett calls poetry in this sequence 'medicated music'. Poetry can find a place for what can otherwise look so small and transitory in the world—a look, a word, a tone of voice—and give such things their true size and meaning. It is as if, in the space between the lover and her addressee, an inner voice of truth has power to reveal itself, at just the right time, to the person who needs it—something like a pure version of what free indirect discourse offers in the novel. For without these moments of triggered surprise Elizabeth Barrett cannot realise her own story as a loved woman—cannot accept this as indeed a love story and a good one. Then Elizabeth Barrett's ability authentically to have her own story can really begin: 'I love thee!'

****

What I am concluding here is that the more vitally transformative personal event at periods of unhappiness, might not be the conventional narrative confession of a 'single story' but the sudden triggered surprise of realization—the version of 'poetry' that those who are not poets experience when their life comes back to them in a sort of revelation of memory. Narrative, I conclude, is not sufficient, may even be distorting.

The concern of the next chapter is with how to get the experience of poetry-like triggers into the world which is not poetry. This means not merely considering how to get the poetic moment accepted as an idea in the context of mental health needs. It really means considering how to get poetry back into the idea of life, and back into use there, as a form of thinking and experiencing vital to human flourishing.

The next chapter will thus be turning to real people reading poetry aloud, live, together, in small groups. I close now with a brief preview of what poetry is in those who are not poets.

Evelyn, now almost sixty and single, has had cerebral palsy from birth. An injury thirty years ago, while caring for her alcoholic mother, left her further disabled. She often feels very alone and describes her sense of loneliness as 'that horrible feeling when you feel you have a ton weight on your chest, as if something is crushing all the feelings out of you'. Here, we see Evelyn reading for the first time Ben Jonson's seventeenth-century poem, *Ode To the immortall memorie, and friendship of that noble paire, Sir Lucius Cary and Sir H. Morison*. It is a poem of consolation to Cary on the death, in his youthful prime, of his friend, Morison:

> life doth her great actions spell,
> By what was done and wrought
> In season, and so brought
> To light: her measures are, how well
> Each syllabe answer'd, and was form'd, how faire;
> These make the lines of life, and that's her aire.
>
> It is not growing like a tree
> In bulke, doth make man better bee;
> Or, standing long an Oake, three hundred yeare,
> To fall a logge, at last, dry, bald, and seare:
> A Lillie of a Day
> Is fairer farre, in May,
> Although it fall, and die that night;
> It was the Plant, and flowre of light.

Evelyn noticed how 'flowre of light', repeated 'brought/to light' from the preceding verse; and how that last line, her favourite in the poem, came after 'die that night'. She said: 'It makes you still see the daytime and the flower – you still see it even though you know it's already dead: "It *was* the Plant", "A Lillie of a Day" '. This is good reading, because Evelyn is in tune with how the poem is holding onto something that the 'season', in its passing, cannot. She also intuits that it is the poem's quietly echoing backward–forward repetitions—light/light, as well as faire/fairer and falls/falls—which delicately counterpoint and minutely halt, just for a second, time's onward movement.

Evelyn herself went on:

> I always have fresh flowers in the house, maybe only a little bunch. But it was what my dad did, for my mother. Sometimes, when I get very depressed I go and do something or think about something where it was happy, before my mum died and things like that. It can be the smallest thing. The other week I was sitting out in the garden one morning early and the lad down the street let his birds out to fly: about a dozen of them, all white, and they were only flying around the roofs, going from his house up to mine and they were circling back, but it was just lovely - it was lovely just sitting watching them glide and they are on the wind, like blossoms.

Such a moment, like the flowers she keeps deliberately in view, help 'remind' Evelyn, as she put it, that 'I have got happiness inside me somewhere locked away'. It is the same with this poem, she said.

What is important here is that the poem is not merely an encouragement to Evelyn to 'remember the good times', 'what was done and wrought'. Rather, it offers a 'reminder' of some present dimension of experience 'locked away' inside which still requires and claims, even amid the bad times, its right expressively to exist—its 'season' in which to be. Even within what Evelyn sometimes feels is her over-prolonged and damaged existence, the poem trips off an alternative scale and 'measure' for the worth of 'the smallest thing'. And, crucially, this quick revaluing of experience is transmitted via the poem's own short, faire-form'd 'lines' and tiny 'syllabes'. As the poem says:

> In small proportions, we just beauties see:
> And in short measures, life may perfect bee.

Longer would spell it out but make it thinner.

Notes

1. Christopher Dowrick, *Beyond Depression*, 2nd ed (Oxford: Oxford University Press, 2009), p. 160.
2. From an interview for the *Student British Medical Journal*, 2011: *Student BMJ* 19:d3338.
3. Iona Heath, 'Divided We Fail': The Harveian Oration, 2011 (London: Royal College of Physicians, 2011), pp. 8–13.
4. Iona Heath, 'Following the Story: Continuity of Care in General Practice' in Trisha Greenhalgh and Brian Hurwitz (eds), *Narrative-Based Medicine* (London: BMJ Books, 1998), pp. 83–92, p. 86.
5. Arthur Kleinman, *The Illness Narratives* (New York: Basic Books, 1988), pp. 60, 87, 253.
6. Oliver Sacks, *The Man Who Mistook His Wife for a Hat* (London: Picador, 1986), p. 105.
7. Oliver Sacks, *The Man Who Mistook His Wife for a Hat* (London: Picador, 1986), pp. 34–5.
8. Suzanne Corkin, *Permanent Present Tense: the Unforgettable Life of the Amnesic Patient H. M.* (New York: Basic Books, 2013), p. 205.
9. Michael Balint, *The Doctor, His Patient and the Illness* (London: Pitman Publishing Ltd, 1957), p. 4. Hereafter *Balint*.
10. Iona Heath, 'Following the Story: Continuity of Care in General Practice' in Trisha Greenhalgh and Brian Hurwitz (eds), *Narrative-Based Medicine* (London: BMJ Books, 1998), pp. 83–92, p. 83.
11. See chapters 11–13 of *The Doctor, His Patient and the Illness* (pp. 107–71) for Balint's discussion of the doctor's 'atmosphere'.
12. Trisha Greenhalgh, 'Narrative Based Medicine in an Evidence-Based World', *Narrative Medicine*, p. 251.
13. Trisha Greenhalgh, 'Narrative Based Medicine in an Evidence-Based World', *Narrative Medicine*, p. 263.
14. Arthur W. Frank, *The Wounded Storyteller* (Chicago: University of Chicago Press, 1995), chapters 1–3.
15. Rita Charon, *Narrative Medicine* (Oxford: Oxford University Press, 2008), p. 269.
16. C. E. Rudebeck, 'The Body as Lived Experience in Health and Disease', in *Medical Humanities Companion*, Volume One: *Symptom*, ed. by Martin Evans, Rolf Ahlzen, Iona Heath and Jane MacNaughton (Oxford: Radclyffe Publishing, 2008): see also Volume Two, *Diagnosis* (2010), pp. 1–3.
17. John Berger, *A Fortunate Man*, 1967 (Cambridge: Granta Books, 1989), pp. 36–7.
18. John Berger, *A Fortunate Man*, 1967 (Cambridge: Granta Books, 1989), p. 37.
19. Christopher Dowrick, *Beyond Depression*, 2nd ed (Oxford: Oxford University Press, 2009), p. 207.
20. Rita Charon, *Narrative Medicine* (Oxford: Oxford University Press, 2008), p. 9.
21. Iona Heath, 'Divided we Fail: The Harveian Oration 2011' (London: Royal College of Physicians, 2011), p. 11.
22. Trisha Greenhalgh and Brian Hurwitz (eds), *Narrative-Based Medicine* (London: BMJ Books, 1998), p. 14.

23. Somewhere between the first and final year of medical education, undergraduate students exchange a native facility for appreciating patients' narratives for the learned expertise of constructing a medical history. 'Interviewing Skills of First-Year Medical Students', *Journal of Medical Education* (1986) 61: 842–4.

24. Michael Balint, *The Doctor, His Patient and the Illness* (London: Pitman Publishing Ltd, 1957), p. 121.

25. Michael Balint, *The Doctor, His Patient and the Illness* (London: Pitman Publishing Ltd, 1957), p. 136.

26. Michael Balint, *The Doctor, His Patient and the Illness* (London: Pitman Publishing Ltd, 1957), p. 121.

27. J. Donald Boudreau, Stephen Liben, Abraham Fuks, 'A faculty development workshop in narrative-based reflective writing', *Perspectives on Medical Education* (2012) 1:143–54 DOI 10.1007/s40037-012-0021-4.

28. John Launer, *Narrative-Based Primary Care* (Oxford: Radclyffe Medical Press Ltd, 2002), Ch 15, pp. 203–14.

29. Michael Balint, *The Doctor, His Patient and the Illness* (London: Pitman Publishing Ltd, 1957), pp. 76–80.

30. Galen Strawson, 'Against Narrativity', *Ratio* (new series), 2004, 14:428–52, p. 447.

31. Hannah Arendt, *Men in Dark Times*, 1968 (London: Penguin Books Ltd, 1973), p. 29.

32. Louise M. Rosenblatt, *Literature as Exploration*, 1938 (New York: The Modern Language Association of America, 1995), p. 38.

33. Trisha Greenhalgh and Brian Hurwitz (eds), *Narrative-Based Medicine* (London: BMJ Books, 1998), p. 6.

34. Rita Charon, *Narrative Medicine* (Oxford: Oxford University Press, 2008), p. i.

35. Wilfred Bion, *Learning From Experience* (London: Maresfield Library, 1989), p. 116.

36. Michael Balint, *The Doctor, His Patient and the Illness* (London: Pitman Publishing Ltd, 1957), p. 172.

37. David J. Linden, *The Accidental Mind* (Cambridge, Mass: Harvard University Press, 2007), pp. 225–32.

38. Chimamanda Adichie, 'The Danger of a Single Story', TED talk, 2009.

39. J. W. Bennett, 'The Apprenticeship of George Eliot: Characterisation as Case Study in *Janet's Repentance*', *Literature and Medicine*, 1990, 9:50–68.

40. Raymond Tallis, 'Language, Literature and Human Consciousness', *The Reader*, 38, 2010, pp. 63–71, p. 66.

41. D. A. Miller, *Jane Austen, or, The Secret of Style* (Princeton: Princeton UP), 2003.

42. See 'The Courtship Correspondence' in Josie Billington and Philip Davis (eds), *Elizabeth Barrett Browning: 21st Century Oxford Authors* (Oxford: Oxford University Press, 2014).

3

Reading in Practice

Finding the Poetry

In a mental health drop-in centre in a northern city, a group of six people are reading together. Among them are: Ron, a thoughtful man in his fifties who had been an avid reader until his wife became seriously ill; Mary, a voluble woman in her eighties, recently widowed; and Linda, educated and in her forties, who often does not speak but sometimes shows quiet signs of distress. The group has been meeting weekly for a number of weeks, sharing fiction and poetry which they read aloud together. The group members are taking part in a research study investigating the benefits of shared reading for people suffering from anxiety or low mood, or other symptoms of what is called 'depression'. It is one of the studies on reading and health being carried out by CRILS, the Centre for Research into Reading, Literature and Society at the University of Liverpool where I and my colleagues in literature, medicine, and psychology are based. We have video-recorded and transcribed some sessions.

Here the group is reading an early sonnet by Elizabeth Barrett Browning. Several years before she met Robert Browning, Elizabeth Barrett's closest brother, Edward, was drowned in a boating accident. The bereavement was so intense and painful that it almost killed her and left her for a long time without the power of words at all. 'I fall into silences now, both of voice & writing,' she wrote almost a year after his death. 'I have written very little poetry. It appears to me early for anyone struck by such a blow, to be able to throw the pang of it into verse.' Elizabeth Barrett's notebooks from this period show the poet trying out the sonnet form for the first time, as if its tightness and brevity were a means to dare back to life a content which her suffering life could barely support.

This poem, 'Grief', is first read aloud by the group leader. She then re-reads the opening:

> I tell you, hopeless grief is passionless—
> That only men incredulous of despair,
> Half-taught in anguish, through the midnight air,
> Beat upward to God's throne in loud access
> Of shrieking and reproach.

A recording and then transcript was made of the group's subsequent discussion. After a short pause, Ron is the first to speak. He finds the poem puzzling at first:

There's so many things. It's, it's disjointed. It - it's not straight-forward is it? You don't look at it and think oh yeah that's that. 'I tell you, hopeless grief is passion...passionless.'

He knows the surprise, the change of word from the obvious, and the shift from the obvious is often a crucial starting point. The poem then speaks not of a desert of feeling, but worse, paradoxically, of 'full desertness'. Then, instead of crying upward to God's throne, this:

> Deep-hearted man, express
> Grief for thy Dead in silence like to death;
> Most like a monumental statue set
> In everlasting watch and moveless wo,
> Till itself crumble to the dust beneath!
> Touch it! the marble eyelids are not wet—
> If it could weep, it could arise and go.

Mary repeats the final line. 'If it could weep, it could arise and go.'

Mary: If it was as simple as, shedding tears, you could kind of get on with it. You could get it over and done with.
Linda: But grief isn't like that is it.... When you use the word grief ... it's something that comes ... you think of something that comes right from inside and down don't you.

This is the moment we as researchers are looking for—when the normal, obvious language of the participants is put under pressure by the imagined event, when it is inflected by the language of poetry. 'Right from inside and down...'. After all the hesitations about what to say, this is a kind of pre-language, getting in earlier to visceral feelings.

What is happening here is that the group, in reading the poem, is doing again what Elizabeth Barrett did in writing it—strugglingly searching for words to express a real content which is almost inarticulable. Through her whole life, Elizabeth Barrett Browning never could speak of her grief, except in her poetry. She needed poetry's creatively structured pressure and she needed its second voice. This instance of reading is a momentary reminder of what poetry is really for: to make what is deeply inner and private, and rarely expressible in normal life, both more personally felt and more publicly sharable.

This awakening is the work of The Reader. Now a national charity, The Reader began life as a small community outreach unit of the School of English at the University of Liverpool, taking serious literature out of the tutorial room and into the world with groups of people who typically were not literature students but who were beginners. Currently there are almost 400 reading groups, not only in schools or libraries or book shops, but oddly or surprisingly in places concerned with health provision: hospitals, GP surgeries, mental health clinics. There is no predetermined agenda; the groups start with a book—a work of fiction or poetry—not with a book prescribed to deal with a specific problem and a check list of desired results. People feel better in a range of ways for joining these groups. It is hard to characterize or define these gains. The Reader's practice fits neither of the categories to which it is apparently most closely allied—education or therapy.

One thing is clear: the effect is to do with both reading aloud *together* and reading *live*.

The following example is from a community group run by The Reader and commissioned by an NHS mental health trust. As throughout this book, the names are fictionalized. The group is reading John Clare's sonnet, 'I Am'. Here are the first twelve lines:

> I am—yet what I am none cares or knows;
> My friends forsake me like a memory lost:
> I am the self-consumer of my woes—
> They rise and vanish in oblivious host,
> Like shadows in love's frenzied stifled throes
>
> And yet I am, and live—like vapours tossed
> Into the nothingness of scorn and noise,

> Into the living sea of waking dreams,
> Where there is neither sense of life or joys,
> But the vast shipwreck of my life's esteems;
> Even the dearest that I loved the best
> Are strange—nay, rather, stranger than the rest.
> (John Clare, 'I Am', 1848)

Mike, a father in his thirties who is a regular attendee and always happy to speak, leaves the room abruptly, immediately after the poem has been read. The group leader is worried that the poem may have had a bad effect. Mike returns twenty minutes or so later when the group is focusing on the concluding six lines of the poem:

> I long for scenes, where man hath never trod
> A place where woman never smiled or wept
> There to abide with my Creator, God;
> And sleep as I in childhood, sweetly slept,
> Untroubling, and untroubled where I lie,
> The grass below – above, the vaulted sky.

'It's like he wants to feel *no* emotion at all—Untroubling, untroubled, un, un,' says Angela, a group member, 'And yet,' adding interestingly, 'the poem's *full* of emotion.' Mike speaks for the first time now, re-reading the penultimate line carefully aloud: 'Untroubled and untroubling where I lie'. Then he says, with visible effort—hesitant: 'It's almost like...he wants freedom from mental turmoil or something like that, you know,...just to not kind of cause any trouble...or feel anything horrible...or anything like that'. This is how hard it can be to translate something deeply and privately personal into outward articulate form.

As part of the study, participants were asked about their experience of reading afterwards at individual interview and were shown highlights from the video-recording in order to help them recall the feel of significant but small passing moments. The interviewer had tactfully chosen not to include Mike's initial reaction to the poem for viewing, but Mike himself brought it up:

Mike: I don't know whether you've got that clip. I wouldn't like to see that as it would set me off again. Reading these things...it does really stir you up. When I was in London I spent years and years and years going to see this therapist. I'm obsessed with context. And she always used to say, whenever I tried to 'place' people and experience: 'That's the sociological defence' whenever she thought I wasn't speaking for *me*. This just took me completely by surprise.

The thing that really set me off is because I... you know... I did actually... you know... I had a nervous breakdown. I've had more than one. An episode of depression—I had a breakdown about five years ago. And reading that poem was like being taken back to it—The words went in and struck something directly... right inside.

There is something remarkable about how these words from another person, living in another time and place, are sensed by Mike as almost physical events. It is as though, when the dumb marks on the page come alive again in spoken performance, what lives also is the unspoken feeling that originally summoned and required those words. For Bion, poetry is almost unique as a container which thus achieves 'durability and extensibility'. Only in 'poetic and religious expression' has 'the carrying power of the statement been extended in time and space'.[1]

The kind of reading witnessed here is as far as it could possibly be from the experience of reading in a modern book club. Book clubs, say their advocates with some justice, perform an important function in contemporary society, in offering, usually to women more than men, a sense of community, some time-out from crowded routines, and a forum for talk which is more 'cooperative than competitive'.[2] But book club members get together to discuss their thoughts *about* a book they have read in advance, not to share the experience *of* it, through live reading aloud. The book club is a meeting group that takes place after the event of reading has been concluded, and where the voice that speaks through the book is customarily submerged or forgotten amid the exchange of preconceived opinion. Where bits of the books are read aloud, they are read and then left. Characteristically, the demand is for quick reads and modern 'relevant' themes, so the books selected are drawn almost exclusively from contemporary fiction.

But if poetry hurts in the way it hurt the man who read John Clare, why would you choose it? Why not opt instead for the relative comfort

of book-club reading? This is the question that the interviewer instinctively put to Mike when he spoke of how the John Clare poem made
him feel, shorn of his sociological defence:

> *Interviewer:* And yet you kept coming to the group...And you
> came back into the room...
>
> *Mike:* I've been to other groups – you know, where you're all
> sitting there because you're ill and talking about how you feel
> terrible, everything's going wrong. Here there were particular
> words—I remember—something about turmoil and being
> tossed on the sea. I'm feeling it now. When it's very close to
> the surface...my emotions I guess are trying to sort of put it
> together. I needed this language. 'I am'—just to say 'I am'—
> that is something isn't it?

The language of support groups was of little use to Mike. Instead a
language to describe subjective experience is what is needed. Yet, says a
contemporary European philosopher, Claire Petitmengin, working in
the area of phenomenology, the science of lived experience, this is just
what we are missing. 'The vocabulary at our disposal to describe the
various dimensions and subtle processes of our subjective lives is very
poor, and this poverty can probably be put down to the fact that in our
culture it has been little explored.'[3] Too often the language of personal
experience is not personal: it is over-familiar, made cliché, or fitted to
contemporary vocabularies and agendas. The underlying rawness is
hard to get down to ('right from inside and down'). It cannot be reflected
upon or verbalized while it is happening, and is often too fleeting to
capture anyway. Subsequent reflection *upon* it always risks distortion *of*
it. In the business of knowing our inner selves, we all are beginners. The
novice readers we have been witnessing might be further on than most,
for not being able to do too much. They don't take it for granted.

Literature is the one area of our inherited culture which *does* seriously explore the inner life. Our customarily impoverished language
for first-person data is exactly why we need poetry's and fiction's ded-
ication to articulate recognition of subjective experience. 'This is me,'
readers sometimes instinctively say. But literature's value is not some
easy autobiographical expressiveness or projection, reading off the
inner life as if from outside. Instead literature offers itself as precisely
the 'trigger' that phenomenological science is looking for to create 'a

relationship of contact with our own inward experience'.[4] It offers what Balint struggled to provide in his doctor's surgery: the right emotional atmosphere in which to hear and to speak.

The following example of this triggering by mental excitement and emotion concerns Lois, a young woman in her early twenties who is attending a community reading group. She is suffering some significant neurological impairment resulting from an accident during a stay in South Africa where she came into devastating contact with an electric fence. The group have been reading Robert Frost's 'The Road Not Taken':

> Two roads diverged in a yellow wood,
> And sorry I could not travel both
> And be one traveler, long I stood
> And looked down one as far as I could
> To where it bent in the undergrowth;
>
> Then took the other, as just as fair,
> And having perhaps the better claim.

In fact both paths, that morning, equally lay open, says Frost:

> Oh, I kept the first for another day!
> Yet knowing how way leads on to way,
> I doubted if I should ever come back.
>
> I shall be telling this with a sigh
> Somewhere ages and ages hence:
> Two roads diverged in a wood, and I –
> I took the one less travelled by,
> And that has made all the difference.

The group talk initially, and conventionally enough, about 'life choices': opting for a school, university, or career; staying in a steady job or risking starting a business. But suddenly, here, for the first time Lois speaks about her accident:

It could be a very minor choice or it could be a very big choice. I mean, for example, a lot of my health problems started when I went to South Africa…but if I hadn't gone I would still probably be like: wanting to go here, want to go there. At the same time I wouldn't have the same…the same problems, as I do now. Would I have the same…mentality as now? Perhaps it

could have been worse. I could have not gone and done something else. Something worse could have happened. Or I could
have been worse if it had been easier.

Up to this point, Lois's response is not going far from the honourable
but conventional norm, as she tries not to 'make too much' of what
happened.

But if anyone was thinking of going and doing exploring...I'd
say, don't do it...don't do this, don't do that, don't do the
other...I'd be awful if if ...I'd be awful if if I ever had, if I ever
had, if if I ever had, if if I ever, if I ever had...children because
I'd be like, you're not doing that.

Four or five times over, that stutter occurs on the 'if', the poem's own
key word ('I doubted if I should ever come back'). Lois's neurological
disability meant that she often had difficulty in concentrating and
occasionally had problems with fluent speech. But it was here that
Lois's intermittent speech problems came under most emotional
strain, repeating 'If I ever had' before managing to complete the
sentence—'children'. We measured it—at no point during the twelve
weeks did her stutter ever last so long. What she knows is that, as a
result of her accident, she is of course unlikely ever to have children,
a partner or family. She has known this, one might guess, for some
time. But there are things one knows which one cannot quite think. So
it comes through the veiled. 'If I ever have...' where 'ever' probably
means 'never'. It is like Angela reading Clare's 'I Am' and seeing on
the other side of the wish for no emotion, very great emotion indeed.

This is not voluntary personal story: it is triggered. This is when a
reader knows something real is happening. In place of the narrative
of literal confession or default biography there is, in Lois at this
moment, something like her poem.

Viewing this moment at interview, another member of the group
said:

The poem makes you think about things on a more...on a level
that you can actually see. In your head you can see what you're
thinking, rather than it just being part of your general feeling on
life. You kind of pinpoint things more. Mostly we are not in the
right place to have the right thought. But reading puts me there.

What poetry is doing in these instances is putting people in a place where something can come of what is not in itself good. I do not say that poetry alone can or should do this. As I have said and as Balint suggested, a doctor's creation of a good personal 'atmosphere' can do much in opening up hidden lives. Yet there is this crucial distinction: where the doctor's duty is to listen, the poet's is to speak. The poet provides for its reader (client, patient, respondent, collaborator) not only the atmosphere but the *language* for release of what would otherwise remain unsayable or reduced to cliché. That language triggers inner echoes, responses triggered and inflected with the emotional vocabulary of the poem.

****

What I want to consider is how fiction and poetry might offer a more emotionally open and more individually precise alternative to programmatic therapies, be they counselling or Cognitive Behavioural Therapy (CBT).

People turn to formal therapy because the right context or right thought does not occur often enough in normal life. Instead there can often seem to be just bad thoughts, sad thoughts, going round and round. In this sense we are all living half-lives most of the time, in need of the good doctor or right atmosphere or whatever can give back to us what we have missed or only half-realized. When we have no other help—no doctor, no friend, no good moment—literature can be a way to retrieve for normal life what is hidden within it. Literature helps to allow the very condition of our not being fully alive for much of the time, precisely by its not being therapy and by its being not-therapy for all.

One good way to see what literature adds to normal half-lives is to see what it does for those lives where the damage is more obvious. Just as neurologists are concerned with the missing parts of the brain in order better to understand what normal functioning is like, so those with explicitly diagnosed mental health issues, though far from brain damaged, offer more manifest versions of what are only our normal worries and ill health, differing most usually in degree, not in kind. Severe mental illness, it is true, might be different in kind from the norm. But even thus at its worse, such illness might show from within an extreme situation what we are hiding in normal ones. Until the last decade, most psychoses were thought untreatable except by drugs. Currently, it is coming to be widely recognized that much mental illness is a result of trauma, of damaging experience. Low mood, unhappiness, loss of sharpness, feeling down, belong to the same family of human experience as the disabling disorientation and suffering that psychiatric medicine treats as 'disease'.

One of our most recent research studies took place at the Royal Liverpool Hospital with chronic pain patients. These are people who attend the pain clinic weekly, not in any expectation of a cure, nor primarily for purposes of medication. In most cases there is no longer one clear physiological cause for their pain. The consultant who runs the clinic does not think of the regular attendees as 'pain patients' but as 'sufferers'. He and his colleagues have long been aware that their role as pain specialists is secondary to their essential one, as of more general practitioners, seeking to help the patient's problem by trying to understand it as part of a human life.

What follows is an excerpt from one of the groups that the clinic runs as part of its 'holistic approach to care'; another phrase better in what it tries to stand for than in its repeated programming. This session is not a literary group in the first instance but forms part of a Cognitive Behavioural Therapy (CBT) programme—the standard psychological treatment for chronic pain, which the consultants have adapted for their patients' particular needs. CBT rests on the premise that a person's thoughts determine his or her feelings and behaviour, and thus a sustained attempt to change and inhibit negative and unhelpful thought patterns is the key to overcoming psychological distress.

There is a strong neurological argument for using this therapy with pain patients. The consultant explains it in lay terms in this session. There are specialized cells in your body, he says, whose job it is to detect and transmit pain and nothing else. Usually pain is picked up by one of these receptors, and impulses are sent through the nervous system to the brain. What happens in people with chronic pain, however, is that other nerves are recruited into this 'pain' pathway which start to fire off messages to the brain when there is no physical stimulus or damage. 'When we look back through case notes for people who have been coming for a long time, we often see that we're treating a different area to the one we were concerned with originally, and that's because the pain wiring system has set itself up and the body's joined in with it.' But the body can 'unjoin' again. Nerve blockers (drugs) are one way; CBT is another—by getting the brain to send new messages back to the body.

There are four patients in the group. In this example two of them stand out. One is Anthony, the other is Susan. It is Anthony, an ex-soldier and once a successful businessman, who most appreciates the idea of 'new messages'. He says that his pain began in his lower limbs and has now moved to his hands and arms so that where he once had a manual wheelchair, he now needs an electric one. He used to spend hours in his workshop until his family decided he was 'doing too much' and sold his tools. Since then he has taken up regular swimming: 'It is my way of reactivating the nerve endings. It's a way to regenerate something.' He goes swimming every day, sometimes for hours, and has lost thirteen stone in weight.

Susan is a young single mother with small children and, by contrast, is absorbed by fears of relapse. 'There's always danger in hope,' she says. 'Just lately, I've been feeling a little bit better, you see. But just seeing a news headline this morning saying "Cold Snap on the Way" filled me with so much horror because I just know I'm going to be in agony.'

At the beginning of the session, the consultant asks: Does anyone else have worries just now? After a pause, Susan says, 'I have worries, yeah':

> *Consultant*: Can anyone tell us more about the worries they have.
> [PAUSE]
> *Susan*: That you're not going to get better.
> *Consultant*: That you're not going to get better.
> *Susan*: I feel it's going to be like this forever. And the degeneration. What I was like two and a half years ago is nothing to the pain I'm feeling now.
> *Consultant*: Yes, there's the getting worse part of it, as well.

There is no prospect of getting better. There is only getting worse, and with no sure end in sight; in terminal illness, as the consultant is acutely aware, for better or worse, there would at least be the certainty of an end very soon. Where this chronic illness is concerned, moreover, there is nothing to be gained by 'fighting it'. On the contrary, the adrenalin produced by the distress of resistance only recreates the pain, as in a vicious circle. For the patient's own sake, the consultant knows, blind resistance needs to be replaced by something closer to tolerant acknowledgement, if at all possible. The only 'hope' is to think differently about what cannot be otherwise changed, using CBT:

Consultant: How do you feel about not getting things back? How do you feel about acceptance?

Susan: I'm not anywhere near—on a scale of 1 to 10, I'd say I'm minus 10.

Change, approached in this direct way, can seem too big a thing to accomplish.

In this comparative research project, a reading group was also running at the clinic concurrently with the CBT group. Over six weeks, patients had been reading Charles Dickens's *A Christmas Carol*. Diane, middle-aged, and a part-time nurse who cares for her elderly parents and grandchildren, had been attending both groups. She had been indifferently attentive over the first few pages of the book, often needing to get up to walk around to relieve discomfort. Scrooge seemed too familiar a character to engage her interest at first.

But Diane became animated at the first sign of something new in Scrooge himself. When the Ghost of Christmas Past returns Scrooge to his boyhood days, it is Diane who re-reads this sentence:

A lonely boy was reading near a feeble fire; and Scrooge sat down upon a form, and wept to see his poor forgotten self as he used to be.

'He weeps for himself,' she says subtly, 'but it's not just self-pity'. Towards the close of the book, the Ghost of Christmas Yet to Come grants Scrooge a vision of his own deathbed—'He lay in the dark empty house, with not a man, a woman, or a child, to say that he was kind'. In another of those turnarounds to which Diane is keenly alert, Scrooge wills a reversal of his fate: 'Assure me that I may yet change these shadows you have shown me by an altered life?' Diane points to the words 'kind' and 'altered' as what she calls mental pain's pressure points:

Diane: Isn't this sort of like someone writing a story, and reading over what they've put in the story and then—[energetically]

> they go back and—and *alter* it. The phantom is showing that
> the future can be changed if it wants to change.
> *Group Leader*: That's a lovely way of putting it, Diane.
> *Diane*: (quoting) 'I hope to live to be another man.'

'And *alter* it' is a message new-fired, like a nerve impulse, its tone and
emphasis triggered by the text's 'change these shadows ... by an
altered life'. Diane thought she knew Scrooge's story as well as she
knew her own. But 'If *it* wants to change' is indeed a lovely and novel
formulation. The invisible future is itself potentially animated here—
if Scrooge can get behind it as it were.

The momentary shift in Diane, away from her default attitude and
usual language, is an involuntary happening, not an intended outcome. It points to one key difference between the therapeutic proper-
ties of reading and the programmatic expectations of formal therapy,
shown in the contrasts in the vocabulary of response. The story begins
to make a change in the reader here precisely by not demanding one
except from Scrooge.

Rhiannon Corcoran, the psychologist on the CRILS research
team, explains the difference like this. CBT works, she says, through
disciplined planned stages, outside of immediate experience, to prevent repetitive thought-patterns. The therapist says, 'Don't dwell on
the bad stuff', 'Look forward – try not to look back'. Reading, by
contrast, is an evolving process where breakthroughs into meaning
happen from within an experience:

> The 'top-down' regulatory basis of CBT, where thinking is origi-
> nally suggested by another and then taken on by the self, may be
> likely to produce only short-lived, 'un-owned' effects. Reading
> works from below upwards. The executive brain gets to work with
> genuine, spontaneous and 'owned' gut- or heart-responses and
> becomes involved in integrating them into models of the world.[5]

In a later CBT session with the same participants as the one described
previously, the consultant concentrated on the importance of recognizing and overcoming 'negative thoughts'. 'It reminds me of being in
the army,' said Anthony:

> *Anthony*: They always talked about negative thoughts and when
> you go into operational theatre you're always told to think

positively. So if you're going down a road and the bridge has been taken out, you were told to think the bridge was still there.

Consultant: Does anyone else have a way of thinking the bridge is still there?

Susan: I take more painkillers so as to be able to work. I always loved my work—catering; it was my life. I came out of an extremely abusive relationship and was free for the first time in eight years. Now I've become trapped by something else. If I could switch it all off and not worry about having to get up and go to work that would be better. But financially it would be crippling. So I'm sort of semi-crippled one way or the other but at least we're living.

Consultant: Crippled is a very strong word.

The consultant is alarmed and his tone is a little admonitory. 'Crippled' feels too negative and the word is not perhaps appropriate for disability.

But contrast some weeks later. Susan has joined the reading group having completed the CBT course and is responding to this passage towards the close of David Guterson's short story, 'Arcturus'. After many years, Carl, the protagonist, has run into Floyd, his boyhood best friend, now 'loused up and rusty...a fat old man'. Carl involuntarily recalls a river trip the two had taken together as adolescents, when he had told Floyd, 'I would die for you. If I ever had to.'

> But now it was night years later. The sun had set already, the stars were out. Nothing is going to change here, Carl thought – even though most things had changed already. And he wished he had never seen Floyd. He wished it had never happened. Nobody needed that kind of reminder. Nobody deserved a jolt like that.

'Isn't that so *sad*,' says Susan, immediately and instinctively, with a quick vivacity of tone. No one would say this immediate reaction is profound thinking—only that it is important first of all to get into the right emotional area and feel it in order *then* to think. Afterwards she recognizes clearly all the reasons why Carl would wish away the jolt: the sight of Floyd, she says, acutely, 'makes him realize how old he is himself'; 'Carl can't reconcile in his mind the way things are to the way things were'. But the emotional energy of her first thought is the opposite of sad or depressed, even though Carl himself feels helpless. The categories of 'positive' and 'negative' are simply not relevant here. She goes back in the text to read this sentence from the preceding paragraph about the river trip the two boys made years ago in adolescence:

> It had been a sweet journey, he thought now. He didn't want to forget about it ever. Even the ridiculous promises had been sweet. He *would* have died for Floyd back then. He'd been dumb enough and young enough for ridiculous things.

Susan disrupts the story's straightforward sequence to bring back what is good even if it never came to pass. 'It's the innocence that he can hardly stand to remember,' she says. This seems an important corrective to the lack of belief in contemporary culture that innocence can be regained, especially if lost and sullied by subsequent trauma. A forensic psychiatrist and research partner of CRILS, Dr David Fearnley, who has run reading groups in the high secure prison where he is based, has ventured that literature's special power, especially when it is read aloud as an emotional–vocal presence, is that it can get underneath habitual categories and frames. It can reach back to a period, a memory, before trauma, before damage set in, as if not everything has to be destroyed by what subsequently happened in life's narrative. The emotion activated is operating at a pre-linguistic level, closer to earlier life, the stage before adult stress patterns took hold or hardened into ill health. So, here, in recovering the innocence, and bearing to do what Carl cannot, it is Susan herself who becomes, momentarily, the protagonist. It is hard to believe she is the same person who had wished to 'switch it all off' in the previous session of CBT. In thus moving one paragraph from its position preceding the later paragraph of regret, she alters the given, won't let the innocence or the memory give way wholly to sad outcomes.

It is the *story* which better achieves CBT's ambition of putting the same person in a different place. Rhiannon Corcoran again:

> It is thought that the human brain is set up as a prediction system to reduce uncertainty. This helps us govern our lives with

least effort and live by routine. Live reading removes the facility
to rely on this 'safe system'. It triggers active happenings and
unpredictable events. Our own experiences are re-felt or
reviewed in a way which challenges habitual emotions or recovers them in a new form.[6]

The power of reading to challenge, ignore, or shift default thinking is
intrinsically connected to literature's broad human range—its abun-
dant inclusion even of what is ostensibly 'negative'.

One great advantage of the shared reading we have been witnessing, is that people have the chance to show and to tell what is usually
private or silent in reading. It is admittedly a different experience from
reading on one's own; but it is the nearest we have for research into
private acts of thinking made live during reading, since the private
here goes on within a group made unusually intimate by the presence
of the poem or short story. What the video recordings make possible
is something unique: it is as if we are able to *see* as well as *hear* people
in the act of suddenly emergent thinking. In fact, that reading is a
special form of thinking is perhaps the most important finding
we have.

So, in what follows, I give two final examples of reading instances
in order to try to get as close as possible to the kind of thinking that
reading finds or helps to create. The examples are taken from the
reading groups once again. But, on this occasion, I have selected
moments of individual rather than group reading. For even this sharing of a book, aloud and together, is always necessarily a form of
personal and individual reading; each member of a reading group, as
Richard Hoggart points out, 'has to try to absorb the book *as if* alone'.[7]

Moreover, the people we witness reading here do not think of
themselves as 'readers' and would not anyway be reading, alone, outside of the group. Sometimes this is related to education or cultural
experience: people assume they are 'not clever enough' to tackle serious books without help. When they do read, the material is usually
magazines, newspapers or the internet; when it is books, popular
romances and thrillers are the standard fare. There is a place for such
'light' reading, but it is not merely condescending to suggest that this
narrow range of genre and the thinness of its quality leaves largely
untapped the latent thinking capacities of modern readers and

severely limits their imaginative exploration of experience. Very often, however, group members—especially those who suffer from anxiety or pain—say they find it difficult to read alone at all due to an inability to concentrate. Susan, whom we just saw re-energized by a short story, had always felt, she said, that 'reading a book was a waste of time because I couldn't take it in'. The reading aloud gives access and initial impetus by offering itself more as life than as a two-dimensional book. Of her experience of shared reading, Susan said:

> From a poem or a story you can get these thoughts in your mind that you wouldn't normally get. You can sort of take them away. What you have tried to absorb can come out later to help you when all these other things are spinning round in your mind that you want to get rid of.

What we see happening in the reading group, therefore, really is these people's version of private reading to which otherwise we have little or no access.

The passage below is from David Constantine's short story 'In Another Country', in which 'a rush of ghosts' enters the life of an elderly married couple, the Mercers. It is now also a film, *45 Years*. The story is this: the body of the husband's first lover, Katya, a Jewish woman whom he had helped to flee from Nazi Germany, has been found preserved in mountain ice 'just the way she was', when he was a young man of twenty. She was Geoff Mercer's first love, pregnant with their child, and she didn't make it. Yet she is preserved in the ice. And the life of her is also preserved all the more in him now, where the sixty years of his childless marriage to Kate seems suddenly not his real life but a mere replacement for what should have been. 'The thing he was most sure about, after all the years, was how sure they were all those years ago that what he wanted with her and she with him was to have a baby and go on living and living together for ever more.' This paragraph occurs as Mr Mercer's time is increasingly spent among photographs and mementos of his first love in the tiny loft 'where the past is stored', the effect on the marriage with Mrs Mercer palpable now as he lives most of his deepest life in that loft:

> They parted company; ate together, slept together but were in separate circles. Almost at once, as though it were beyond his

failing strength, he gave up pitying his wife and fell back down the decades into the couple of months of a summer in the Alps. The ladder to the loft was permanently down, encumbering the way into the little living room. A breath of cold hung over the opening. Or the warmth of their living space, being drawn up there, was converted into cold just above their heads. In the mechanism of her love and duty she called him down when his meal was on the table. But also at nights he went up there and she heard him moving and muttering over the bedroom ceiling. Then she wept to herself, for the unfairness. Surely to God it wasn't much to ask, that you get through to the end and looking back don't fill with horror and disappointment and hopeless wishful thinking? All she wanted was to be able to say it hasn't been for nothing, it hasn't been a waste of time, the fifty years, that they amount to something.

The reader called Mike says of this:

> I don't know how she could have helped him. Or approached it differently so that they wouldn't have separated into their own circles. I mean she's doing her . . . she's doing her duty, she's feeding him, and, you know, they're sharing a bed. She hasn't steamed off in a rage. It's him who's separated from her and in a sense the tragedy is that he couldn't help her either. You know he didn't ask to be . . . to have this memory suddenly rammed down his throat.

'I don't know how she could have helped him'; 'the tragedy is that he couldn't help her *either*'. There is not one thought, here, but two thoughts almost simultaneously; and they are not imposed from without but emerge from the felt space *between* the wife who cannot help her husband and the husband who cannot help his wife. That is a reader's space. It is one of those thought-spaces which literature makes room for, as we saw in *The Death of Ivan Ilyich*, where ordinary life often cannot. This thinking is emotionally loyal to the hidden grammar of the story's paragraph, holding two people at once together and apart, because, at this moment, Mike is instinctively thinking not just as a reader but as a novelist would do. He becomes the thought between the couple—in order to witness and hold it.

This in-between thinking is utterly distinct not only from the top-down procedures of programmatic therapy but from the standard therapeutic uses of fiction in mental health care. Stories, in the latter case, are offered as practical models of individual human situations for the sake of subsequent problem-*solving*. We 'identify' with characters simply in order to 'learn' afterwards by their example.

But the kind of learning going on in Mike is much closer to that which happens, says Bion, when we tolerate frustration. Bion means by this not merely ambiguity or uncertainty, but the bearing of reality itself—of what cannot *be* resolved or got over, but only temporarily held together, in the moment. 'What am I going to do about it?' Mr Mercer asks himself, aloud. 'Nothing. What can I do about it?'

This is why Mike's 'literary-inflected' thinking is so important here: because it is not merely aesthetic—that is, not something unconnected to life. But in life, the situation of husband and wife in Constantine's tale would normally put you on one side or the other, safely limited to one 'character' or another, not placed more riskily in the richly full human matter in-between them.

In fact, the most compelling thinking we see in these recordings happens most often in the area created *between* reader and book, not in any straightforward identification between reader and character or situation. The poet is a 'medicine-man', says Kenneth Burke, 'insofar as his situation overlaps upon our situation . . . is felt by us to be relevant'.[8] 'Overlap' is a much more accurate way of putting it than 'identifying with'. For there is no tidy alignment of story with the reader's personal experience. There is nothing safe about this at all.

Anthony, who has also joined the group following CBT, said in response to the same passage from the Constantine story:

> Some thoughts aren't real are they? Or you don't know whether they're real or not, especially when you're thinking about the past.

This from a man in CBT who knew very clearly what 'positive thinking' was.

> *Anthony*: When I was a child I used to like it when the ice came. I used to think the ice kept things safe.
> *Group Leader*: Why, was that to do with something you had lost?
> *Anthony*: Yes [rubs his face and looks down, no longer smiling]

Anthony was a model CBT student, well in advance of the course in so far he had already established a disciplined self-help regime. But what happens here is a sign that Anthony's real thoughts lie outside, anterior to, the purview of self-regulation and conscious control. Beyond and after his managing to get by, he needs something deeper. Significantly, it is when Anthony has completed treatment and has been 'cured' by CBT—the point at which he is like everybody else— that he finds he needs something else to get further down to where the real problem is. The silence yawns open around that 'Yes'—full of something amorphously bigger and emotionally more powerful than can be fitted into Anthony's usual verbal facility or the standard precepts of a therapeutic programme. But the 'Yes' is spoken, just. Something subterranean, some residuum of experience seems unconsciously to seek, in these few brief seconds, a form of realization that does not simply freeze it and lose it again.

The things that matter to our existence 'leap out' at us, said Heidegger.[9] So with these readers: the personal relevance reveals itself whether they are looking for it or not. This is why the current trend for 'prescribing' certain relevant works for given conditions is both misguided and doomed to failure. *The Novel Cure* half-jokingly describing itself as 'a medical handbook', cites specific novels as remedies for ailments as various as eating disorders, caring for ageing parents, and arrogance. It recommends, for example, Milan Kundera's *The Unbearable Lightness of Being* for periods of clinical depression, the opening of Henry James's *The Portrait of a Lady* for anxiety, William Faulkner's *As I Lay Dying* for inability to express emotion.[10] Such 'treatment'—bibliotherapy as the authors call it—is unlikely to do harm and just conceivably may do some good. But the activation of good moments that we have witnessed in this chapter has occurred because neither the book nor the reader has set aims or outcomes in mind. The poems and stories are not pre-selected with a view to a prescribed effect on a particular client-group— 'depressives' or 'chronic pain sufferers'. The unpremeditated nature of the encounter is what matters: the poem's language finds the person in a deep sense and at a deep level, beneath the stereotype diagnosis or formulaic case.

****

The inner life might always have to be discovered thus involuntarily, triggered from the outside-in, if it is to be retrieved authentically. In the ordinary course of things, people do not have, any more than did Ivan Ilyich, the inclination or encouragement to listen to an inner voice. In times of distress, we hardly know how to trust that voice even if it is available to us. When it is there, it might produce only what psychologists call rumination—the compulsive going over and over, round and round the causes and symptoms of a bad emotional state in ways which intensify depressive mood. More often than not the voice of the inner life has been replaced anyway by a pre-packaged or over familiar version of the personal.

But literature does something deeper still than *recover* an inner voice. It can summon a voice that does not exist under the ordinary conditions of life. 'The business of art,' said Tolstoy famously, 'consists precisely in making understandable and accessible that which might be incomprehensible and inaccessible in the form of reasoning'. 'Usually when a person receives a truly artistic impression, it seems to him he knew it all along, only he was unable to express it'.[11] This is not simply a Tolstoyan prosaic version of Pope's often-quoted but much misunderstood definition of poetry as 'What oft was thought, but ne'er so well express'd'.[12] For what is now known or thought by the reader has not simply preceded the expression of it. It is not consciously *there* until the book, in the very unfolding of its explicit formulation in the reader's mind, finds the implicit and inarticulate matter that was, only half-consciously, in latent need of such release.

Where, for example, does Anthony's devastating 'yes' come from when he answered the group leader: 'Was your sense that ice kept things safe to do with something you had lost?' 'Yes.' Whatever he is privately thinking of comes not simply from 'in his head'; but not just from 'in' the book either. Reality itself at this moment happens in the surprised overlap and movement between the two. As soon as the thought *is* there, however, it is there for *you*. It leaps out, *if* you need it, *when* you need it. This is why the same book can speak to us with new freshness and excited meaning at different stages of a life. But its message is often going backwards or inwards to something previously latent or missing.

In her sonnet sequence, *Later Life,* the religious poet, Christina Rossetti, wrote of this experience from the point of view, of course, of a writer, not a reader:

> We lack but cannot fix upon the lack
> Not this, not that, yet somewhat certainly.

'Somewhat *certainly.'* This is an important clue to what poetry can help to do for its writers *and* its readers alike. For this poem cannot fulfil the lack it expresses; no more can it specify—'fix upon' 'this' or 'that'— just what it is that is missing. What it can strenuously do is underwrite the intuitive certainty of an inner need and longing, the vague sense of lack made at least definite, certain. It's like braille—'not this', 'not that', 'yet somewhat'.

Such inner speaking in the dark is perhaps literature's single most important gift to the modern individual. For, in a secular world, there is nothing external to verify the intuition of another dimension of existence—what Matthew Arnold called the buried life:

> often, in the din of strife,
> There rises an unspeakable desire
> After the knowledge of our buried life;
> A thirst to spend our fire and restless force
> In tracking out our true, original course;
> A longing to inquire
> Into the mystery of this heart which beats
> So wild, so deep in us—to know
> Whence our lives come and where they go.

'To know': that verb lies stranded at the penultimate line-ending. All its urgency for an object is baulked by the questioning indeterminacy that follows—'whence', 'where'. One feels the energy itself 'go' when only the rhyme and nothing more is fulfilled in the succeeding line. But poetry's job isn't just to intimate that somehow, 'somewhat', a deeper life does indeed exist, or to replicate on a reader's behalf the experience of unrealized potential. When a literary work really speaks to someone personally, it offers a tantalizing echo or trace of some layer felt as essential yet eluding definition or revelation:

> And we have been on many thousand lines,
> And we have shown, on each, spirit and power;

> But hardly have we, for one little hour,
> Been on our own line, have we been ourselves—
> Hardly had skill to utter one of all
> The nameless feelings that course through our breast,
> But they course on for ever unexpress'd.

'Hardly', 'hardly', 'one little', 'one of all' 'For ever un-.' This sense of the 'nameless' is not a failure of language merely, any more than it was words that failed Ivan Ilyich in the face of death. The problem here is that this namelessness is one that belongs to human life, and belongs only to it; and yet it, too—like Ivan Ilyich's dying—is a thought which is impossible for human thinking. The deepest truth about us is the very truth we *cannot* fully know. This, says Matthew Arnold, is by design. Fate foresaw by what distractions and strife man would willingly be possessed, even 'well-nigh change his own identity', in order to 'keep from his capricious play/His genuine self'; thus, by way of protecting the authenticity of the inner life, Fate

> Bade through the deep recesses of our breast
> The unregarded river of our life
> Pursue with indiscernible flow its way;
> And that we should not see
> The buried stream.

The goal of the modern secular world—the finding of personal 'identity'—would have seemed to Arnold not only utterly hopeless but, rightly and intentionally, beyond human doing.

Yet perhaps this unreachable or unknowable sense of 'our own line' somewhere is not itself unusual. My own inner life, I often feel, was created in the interstices of family life—which was a good one: normal and loving, nothing terrible. But I was, by some years, the youngest of siblings already almost adult as I was growing up. My brothers and sisters were exceeding my parents, socially and educationally, as my parents had always intended that they should. Again, this was entirely normal, historically, for this generation. Yet I saw it and felt helpless and hurt for my parents. I was conventionally quiet as a child—too quiet, relatives and teachers said, 'lacking in confidence'. For whatever there was to say could be said least of all by me, the youngest member of the family. Those older thoughts seemed out of place in my young self.

But what they made me was the repository of what was going on, and of what was left behind, when my siblings were no longer at home. In such circumstances, what you become is the witness—protectively silent, not wanting to say all you see. Above all, what you are doing is reading the situation, noticing meaning that others, unnoticing, walk away from. This 'reading' or witnessing—hearing a pain in others which was never quite expressed—became 'my line'. It was a submerged inner commentary, sunk down but present—the subterranean thinking which makes me now relish its equivalent in the free indirect discourse of the novel.

It was much later that I realized that the witness—the one who quietly 'thinks' the thoughts implicit in a situation—is of value, even where, perhaps especially where, the wrong cannot practically be put right. What I had experienced as a disadvantage—being, redundantly or misplacedly, the 'noticer' among the family—was, I came to understand, actually a position I could occupy, a role or *métier*. I was a reader outside books as well as in them. That kind of 'reading', as a form of recognition and of repair, is, after all, what George Eliot above all writers represents. In seeing the deep reality which, she says, most humans 'cannot bear', she is also rescuing it from waste merely. 'But hardly have we, *for one little hour*,/ Been on our own line...been ourselves'.

Poetry and fiction, I am saying, are our nearest and best approximation to 0—Bion's truest reality—and the strongest intimation we have for trusting that 0 is there, even for the little hour of a poem or a reading group. Literature gives us not only the thoughts that we don't dare or can't bear to have. Literature gives us also the thoughts we do want—in my case, in youth, thoughts that offered some saving love and value plus the recognition that I could provide them without sadness.

What this reading voice seems to call into being is a psychic or mental equivalent of George Eliot's free indirect discourse in treating of her characters: their own line. A descendant of ancient confession, it is a most powerful tool fiction has for catching elusive and unspoken forms of reality—thoughts barely half-thought yet somewhat there certainly.

As a brief reminder of how this discourse works, here is the close of the climactic chapter in Dorothea's story in *Middlemarch* where Casaubon

has learned that he will soon die. Dorothea has offered to him her
loving pity for his sorrow, but has been coldly repulsed by her husband, and feels a rebellious anger stronger than any she has felt since
her marriage day. 'Was it her fault that she had believed in him – had
believed in his worthiness? – And what exactly was he? In the misera-
ble light she saw her own and her husband's solitude – how they
walked apart so that she was obliged to survey him. If he had drawn
her towards him, she would never have said "Is he worth living for?"'
It is a terrible subvocal question. But then something else springs up
in answer from within:

> The energy that would animate a crime is not more than is
> wanted to inspire a resolved submission, when the noble habit
> of the soul reasserts itself. It cost her a litany of picture sorrows
> and of silent cries that she might be the mercy for those sorrows –
> but the resolved submission did come; and when the house was
> still, and she knew it was near the time when Mr Casaubon
> habitually went to rest, she opened her door gently and stood
> outside in the darkness waiting for his coming upstairs with a
> light in his hand. If he did not come soon she thought that she
> would go down and even risk incurring another pang. She
> would never again expect anything else. But she did hear the
> library door open, and slowly the light advanced up the stair-
> case without noise from the footsteps on the carpet. When her
> husband stood opposite to her, she saw that his face was more
> haggard. He started slightly on seeing her, and she looked up at
> him beseechingly, without speaking.
>
> 'Dorothea!' he said, with a gentle surprise in his tone. 'Were
> you waiting for me?'
>
> 'Yes, I did not like to disturb you.'
>
> 'Come, my dear, come. You are young, and need not to
> extend your life by watching.'
>
> When the kind quiet melancholy of that speech fell on
> Dorothea's ears, she felt something like the thankfulness that
> might well up in us if we had narrowly escaped hurting a lamed
> creature.

What makes this famous moment so great? It is not that something is
finally fulfilled between this couple. It is too late for the drama of full

reconciliation or even for adequate reparation. The best we can say is that what happens does no harm and that that is an achievement. George Eliot knows it is. From 'she felt' in that final paragraph, we feel a thankfulness and sense of relief analogous to Dorothea's own when we hear the kind quiet melancholy of George Eliot's voice speaking for Dorothea what is called in the Bible the thoughts of her heart. But George Eliot's voice is really summoned here by Dorothea's very need to give thanks, as if in prayer, though to no one and for precious little. Not for nothing the religious language in this passage—'it cost her a litany of sorrows'. Yet who is Dorothea to give thanks to at this moment if not her own best self? And that is the very self which only the author—the creator and not the creature—can wholly see. George Eliot occupies at this moment what she calls elsewhere 'the merciful eyes of solitude looking on through the ages at spiritual struggles of man'. She does so in order to give verbal recognition to feelings and thoughts which otherwise have no place in the world. This is the voice that does not exist in ordinary existence, where we do not hear the inner voices inside other people, any more than we can fully hear our own.

We have begun to hear that voice inside these readers—from Evelyn's lyricism at the close of my last chapter to Anthony's pained struggle with speaking in this one. This is the voice that fiction and poetry can help us to get at in ourselves and better hear in others.

Free indirect discourse, to repeat D. A. Miller's formulation, is the character's life as he or she cannot fully live it. Literary reading, we might say, is a person's life as he or she cannot fully *think* it, until the right book comes along.

****

My point in this chapter is not simply that shared and live reading groups are a good thing; my real claim is that everybody needs the 'something deeper' which reading gives. The reading groups remind us, from within ordinary lives, what literature is *for*. And, in thus showing what literature can really do, these instances of personal reading also show what is absent from most current reading practices.

Perhaps we should not need the reminder which these examples from novice readers have given. The reading of serious literature of the past might have become remote from much of modern life, but arguably, whatever the insular downsides, it has been protected in university English departments for the last century. English Literature is still the strongest recruiter in Higher Education among humanities subjects. Yet, what literature really exists to do in the outside world has often become more trapped, even lost, within the academic discipline that was meant to preserve it. Careful reading has either become an emotionless critical 'technique' or has been replaced entirely by the mediation of literary theory and historical context. 'Teachers and students read the great songs and stories to learn *about* them, not to learn *from* them,' says Wendell Berry. 'The texts are tracked as by the passing of an army of ants, but the power of songs and stories to affect life is still little acknowledged, apparently because it is little felt.'[13] If literary reading does not begin with what is personally felt, if people are not 'in place' emotionally when they read, then what literature is for will be forever lost.

In all this, my concern is not with preserving literature just for its own sake. In *Why Be Happy When You Could Be Normal?*, Jeanette Winterson writes of how, growing up under the charge of a fanatically religious adoptive mother, she found in all the great works of literature 'a tough language' to support a tough and damaged life. One winter's night, Mrs Winterson found the books Jeanette had hidden beneath her mattress, threw them from the window and set light to them in the yard:

> I watched them blaze and blaze and remember thinking how
> warm it was, how light, on the freezing Saturnian January night.
> And books have always been light and warmth to me.[14]

Light and warmth! The 'normal' response would have been anger. Instead, she finds the burning books giving back to her something of what they had always secretly given—a power now translated, almost miraculously, into a vital poetic image. There is nonetheless, in this happening, something of the ancient biblical puritanism of book-burning. But again the response is not devastation: 'The books were gone, but they were objects: what they held was already *inside* me.' She is going to write some of those lost books. What is left is pure essence— what Winterson calls elsewhere the inner 'pearl lining' which books protectively deposit. 'You have taken in more than you know, and it will go on doing its work.'[15]

Winterson is lucky in the sense that she could use her bad experience as a writer. Those of us who are not writers still need books as she once rawly did. The biggest risk of all is that the deeper reality, which books hold *for* people, will be 'inside' nobody if the practice of serious reading becomes obsolete.

My concern in Chapter Two was that medical humanities runs the risk very often of instrumentalizing literature. Making literature useful can be its own form of forgetting its real uses. It is a difficult balancing act. In my own research into the mental health benefits of reading, I have experienced at first hand the tension between the will of health sciences, on the one hand, to regard reading instrumentally, as a 'cure' or 'therapy', and the purism of literary studies, on the other, which regards the notion of literature as humanly useful as a form of reductivism. That is the devil and the deep blue sea, the rock and the hard place, where literature actually occupies subtler territory.

Notes

1. Wilfred R. Bion, *Attention and Interpretation* (London: Maresfield Library, 1970), pp. 1–2.
2. Jenny Hartley, *The Reading Groups Book* (Oxford: Oxford University Press, 2002), p. 137.
3. Claire Petitmengin, 'Describing one's subjective experience in the second person: An interview method for the science of consciousness', *Phenomenology and the Cognitive Sciences*, 2006, 5 (3–4): 229–69, pp. 238–9.
4. Claire Petitmengin, 'Describing one's subjective experience in the second person: An interview method for the science of consciousness', *Phenomenology and the Cognitive Sciences*, 2006, 5 (3–4): 229–69, p. 256.
5. See Philip Davis, Josie Billington, Rhiannon Corcoran, Victorina Gonzalez-Diaz, Sofia Lampropoulou, Grace Farrington, Fiona Magee, and Erin Walsh (2015), 'Cultural Value: Assessing the intrinsic value of The Reader Organization's Shared Reading Scheme', p. 41 https://www.liverpool.ac.uk/media/livacuk/instituteof psychology/CV,value,of,RO,shared,reading,scheme.pdf (accessed 27/3/16).
6. See Philip Davis, Josie Billington, Rhiannon Corcoran, Victorina Gonzalez-Diaz, Sofia Lampropoulou, Grace Farrington, Fiona Magee and Erin Walsh (2015), 'Cultural Value: Assessing the intrinsic value of The Reader Organization's Shared Reading Scheme', p. 10 https://www.liverpool.ac.uk/media/livacuk/institute-ofpsychology/AHRC_Cultural_Value_Report.pdf? (accessed 27/3/16).
7. Richard Hoggart, 'Literacy is not Enough' in *Between Two Worlds* (London: Aurum Press, 2001), p. 199.
8. Kenneth Burke, *The Philosophy of Literary Form* (Berkeley: University of California Press, 1967), p. 64.

9. Martin Heidegger, *Being and Time*, (Wiley-Blackwell, 1978), p. 103.

10. Ella Berthoud and Susan Elderkin, *The Novel Cure: An A-Z of Literary Remedies* (Edinburgh: Cannongate, 2013).

11. Leo Tolstoy, *What is Art?*, 1898, trans. Richard Pevear (Harmondsworth: Middle-sex: Penguin Books Ltd, 1995), p. 81.

12. Alexander Pope, *Essay on Criticism*, 1711.

13. Wendell Berry, *Standing on Earth* (Ipswich: Golgonooza Press, 1991), p. 185.

14. Jeanette Winterson, *Why Be Happy When You Could Be Normal?* (London: Jonathan Cape, 2011), pp. 40–3.

15. Jeanette Winterson, *The Guardian*, 31 March 2007.

4

Reading for Life

In one way this book has been on the side of medical humanities, and in another way it hasn't. In its commitment to connecting literature and life, medical humanities is in some senses a more congenial place to reside for someone like myself, who cares about literature's having a place in the world but can find no home either for literature, or for such caring, in existing disciplinary structures. Existing between arts and science, and between the academy and the world, medical humanities is uniquely positioned to re-humanize literature by getting it out of its stuckness within a discipline and by renewing its original purposes as a help for people in trouble. For some good reasons and some bad, literary scholars are concerned about literature's being made merely instrumental, a prop to a health agenda of targets and outcomes. Nonetheless, Medical Humanities has taken an important step forward in making a powerful case for the usefulness of literature. I have argued that the truest usefulness depends upon deep reading, not just surface relevance, both to fulfil literature's wide human utility and to avoid its parasitic appropriation.

What I want to offer in this final chapter is further insistence on the uses of deep reading, and to suggest a further step forward in respect of literature's occupying a place in the world. I argue for the practice of such serious and active reading as an essential part of the education of literature undergraduate students *inside* universities, in order that such practice can act in the service of life *outside* academia.

The work I take as a touchstone for this chapter is again John Berger's masterpiece *A Fortunate Man: The Story of a Country Doctor* to which I referred in Chapter Two. I choose this work for two key reasons.

The first reason is historical. Published in 1967, *A Fortunate Man* is one of the foundational texts for medical humanities. The book explicitly comes out of the work and thought of Michael Balint. Its

subject, Dr John Sassall, a GP in a remote rural practice, is a disciple
and an embodiment, Berger acknowledges, of Balint's 'brilliant'
understanding of what is really demanded of a general diagnostician:
that he search not for a specific condition, case or cure, but for the
whole truth about a person. To the modern day GPs whom we encountered in Chapter Two—Iona Heath and Christopher Dowrick—*A
Fortunate Man* has offered an original model and vital reminder of first
principles.

The second reason is that *A Fortunate Man* is a pioneer in the shift of
literature toward life. A collaboration with the photographer, Jean
Mohr, the work is a ground-breaking photo-documentary—part doc-
umentary case study, part biography, part novel, part philosophical
meditation. This generic mix is the formal outcome of the real
achievement of this work. *A Fortunate Man* represents the creation of a
new hybrid. It uses the resources of fiction in relation to a real-life
subject matter which is not invented as it would be in a novel. In that
way, the book cannot wholly control the material taken from the life
of Sassall, which thus keeps its raw and stubborn recalcitrance. 'I wish
I could write a conclusion summing up and evaluating what has been
noticed,' Berger writes at the close of *A Fortunate Man*:

> But I cannot. It is beyond me to conclude. Sassall's situation can
> only be judged in relation to the work he does in it. And I can-
> not evaluate that work as I could easily do if he were a fictional
> character. In fiction, outcomes can be decided. Whereas now
> I can decide nothing. I am entirely at the mercy of realities
> I cannot encompass.[1]

'I cannot', 'It is beyond me', 'At the mercy of realities'. Berger wel-
comes these failures because he does not want this work to be valued
merely as a closed fiction, a constraining container, as Bion might say.
His not being able to conclude is a way of leaving both the subject
matter and the artefact open. *A Fortunate Man* cannot be simply fenced
in, as 'art'.

It is through this brave and seminal text that I try to see an image of
the kind of mixture of literature with life that is my main concern.

Early in his career, Sassall had seen himself primarily as a life-saver.
He had grown up on the books of Joseph Conrad and the doctor he
aspired to be was a kind of heroic Master Mariner, whose commanding

authority was also in the service of the people who depended upon him. His chief interest was in one-off practical emergencies—performing appendix and hernia operations on kitchen tables, delivering babies in caravans. He sought out accidents and crises of dangerous illness where the patient's condition was simplified to a verifiable external problem requiring immediate practical and precise medical treatment.

Over time, as Sassall was called out frequently to the same homes, the same people, he began to take a different view of crisis and of illness. His patients, he found, made confessions to him for which there was no medical reference, and where no previous explanation would exactly fit. What was wrong depended upon the history of the patient's particular personality and circumstances in life. He very seldom sent a patient to mental hospital, considering it a kind of abandonment. His principal duty, as he saw it, was rather to 'keep that personality company in its loneliness'. What Sassall 'treated' was unhappiness:

> The unhappy patient has failed to find any confirmation of himself in the outside world. In the light of the world he is nobody: by his own lights, the world is nothing. Clearly the task of the doctor – unless he merely accepts the illness at face value and incidentally guarantees for himself a 'difficult' patient – is to *recognize* the man. If the man can begin to feel recognized – and such recognition may include aspects of his character which he has not yet recognized in himself – the hopeless nature of his unhappiness will have been changed. (p. 75, my emphasis)

Just as the doctor exists here to recognize the patient, so the novelist, Berger, writing *A Fortunate Man* exists to recognize the doctor and his work.

The book opens with a series of short case histories. In one of the first of these, Berger recounts Sassall's attendance at the home of a bereft husband following the death of an elderly mother and wife:

> In the parlour the old man rocked on his feet. The doctor deliberately did not put out a hand to steady him. Instead he faced him.

The older man was taller by nine inches. The doctor said quietly, his eyes extra wide behind his spectacles, 'It would have been worse for her if she'd lived. It would have been worse.'

He might have said that there have been kings and presidents of republics who have never recovered from the death of their wives. He might have said that death is the condition of life. He might have said that man is indivisible and that, in his view, this was the only sense in which death could have no dominion.

But whatever he said at that moment, the old man would have continued to rock on his feet, until the daughter lowered him into his chair in front of the unlit fire. (p. 29)

Sassall's duty of care to his patient at this moment is to bear to do and to say nothing, *intentionally*—'the doctor deliberately did *not* put out hand to steady him'. Tacit austerity and the discipline of witnessing take the place of conventional comfort or empathy: 'Instead he faced him'. Analogously, recognition, in Sassall's sense, means doctor and patient 'facing' an area where simple active cure does not apply. It doesn't matter what the doctor actually says—he might have said this, might have said that cliché or space-filler. The fact of his standing it, being a silent attending container for the man's grief, is what is important.

But it does matter that this witness is a silent *language*, and one that only literature can speak of without violating it. Sassall begins where cure cannot operate, Berger, where normal language cannot work. The reason we need literature, to reiterate Iona Heath's words, is because it 'allows no room to good intentions or wishful thinking'.

The two—doctor and writer—are clearly analogous. For one thing, Berger sees how Sassall is working as a sort of practical novelist in real life, imagining and recognizing his people. In the strange condition of modern life, the doctor has to be too many things—between medic, therapist, counsellor, priest, confessor, novelist. But most of all, he is this:

Sassall does more than treat [his patients] when they are ill: he is the objective witness of their lives. He represents their lost possibility of understanding. He also represents some of what they know but cannot think. (p. 109)

Like the novelist, like Bion, he is translating what people are and what they suffer into thoughts that they can think:

> When patients are describing their conditions or worries to Sassall, instead of nodding his head or murmuring 'yes', he says again and again 'I know', 'I know'. He says it with genuine sympathy. Yet it is what he says while he is waiting to know more. He already knows what it is like to be this patient in a certain condition: but he does not yet know the full explanation of that condition, nor the extent of his own power. (p. 81)

This isn't knowingness. What Sassall is very riskily doing is impersonating—'becoming'—his patients. The stamina required for this is incalculable, and the strain is immense. Sassall allows every touch he lays upon his patient and every word his patient speaks to transmit meaning. 'Once he was putting a syringe deep into a man's chest. "That's where I live where you're putting that needle in." "I know," Sassall said, "I can't bear anything done near my eyes. I think that's where I live"' (p. 50). At such moments, what the person is, the place where he or she 'lives', comes through Sassall's own body.

But Sassall also 'waits' for this knowledge to come through his body *and into his mind*—in order, that is, to give what he knows back to his patient. He articulates what the patient is feeling and thinking by proxy. Sassall acts as the benign container, as Bion would say, which holds what is vital in his people for as long as he can, translating their mute experience into himself and into what he can then articulately represent for them. He writes their book, he lets them read it through him, as it were.

'True translation,' Berger recently wrote, 'is not a binary affair between two languages':

> True translation demands a return to the pre-verbal, to what lay behind the words of the original text before it was written. One reads and re-reads the words of the original text to penetrate through them, to reach, to touch, the vision or experience that prompted them. One gathers up what one has found there and takes this quivering almost wordless 'thing' and places it behind the language it needs to be translated into. And now the principal

task is to persuade the host language to take in and welcome the
'thing' that is waiting to be articulated.[2]

So, a book—this book of Berger's—is like what Sassall serves as being
for his patients: it is a container to take in and recreate within itself the
human content that is in need of translated recognition, holding it for
longer than humans ordinarily can.

Yet Sassall's task is itself more than the man himself can contain
wholly or for long. Fifteen years after the publication of *A Fortunate
Man*, John Sassall took his own life. Berger had somewhat antici-
pated this outcome in his account of the prolonged periods of deep
depression that the doctor suffered, triggered by the recognition
that, in trying to cure his patients' suffering, their personal-social
disadvantages, he had bitten off far more than he could chew. The
extent of their multifaceted deprivation was beyond his power to
alleviate or amend. Yet, in an afterword to an edition of *A Fortunate
Man* published a decade after Sassall's death, Berger stated that it
was simply too easy to count Sassall's life a failure because of his
suicide, merely judging his achievement in terms of its after effects
and final outcome:

> Our Instant-Hedonist culture tends to believe that a suicide is a
> negative comment. What went wrong? it naively asks. Yet a sui-
> cide does not necessarily constitute a criticism of the life being
> ended; it may belong to that life's density. This was the tragic
> Greek view. John the man I loved killed himself. His death has
> made his life more mysterious. Not darker.[3]

The book still hands on that life of Sassall's, despite his own ending.
And in this way, the open and hybrid nature of *A Fortunate Man* is
explicitly seeking 'translation' into another person, life or practice—in
the reader. But this is a work which is only showing what all serious
books really exist to do, however formally closed they may look or
may have become within a closed-off discipline. Literature is not a
conclusion but an incitement, said Proust.[4] Literature continually
seeks a place of re-entry, within life, for the messy and burgeoning life
content it cannot resolve or finish. It demands transmission, somewhere else to go, someone to be its carrier.

****

I want to give one or two final concrete examples of what this transmission is like, where a meaning is picked up: a moment when the
preverbal content of a text is delivered to someone who can receive it.

The subject, Jim, a father in his forties, is a member of the chronic
pain reading group discussed in Chapter Three, debilitated by a long-
term condition for which there is no obvious physical cause. His doctor
says people like Jim are not patients, but sufferers. He is quietly spoken
and always appears relaxed, easy-going. On only one previous occasion did Jim's demeanour visibly change, in response to an Elizabeth
Bowen story, 'The Visitor'. A young boy watches the hands of a clock
move round and round, waiting to note accurately the hour and minute when he will be told the news he is expecting: his mother's death.
'I used to look at the clock when I was a child and try to will the second
hand to stop,' said Jim. 'Was that because of something you didn't
want to happen?' the group leader asked. Jim, barely nodding, covered
his face with his hand, in some distress. In reading groups, there are
private moments like this when something is manifestly happening
inside the participant. The group leader knows that she will have to
wait for it to re-surface another time in relation to another text.

A few weeks later, the chronic pain group was reading Doris
Lessing's *A Sunrise on the Veld*, a short story in which a fifteen-year-old
teenager, hunting before dawn with all the courage and excitement of
his youth, hears a terrifying scream of pain. He finds a small animal,
a trapped and injured buck, writhing and jerking convulsively as it is
eaten by ants:

> It grew quieter. There were small twitches from the mass that
> still looked vaguely like the shape of a small animal.
>
> It came into his mind that he should shoot it and end its pain;
> and he raised the gun. Then he lowered it again. The buck
> could no longer feel; its fighting was a mechanical protest of the
> nerves. But it was not that which made him put down the gun.
> It was a swelling feeling of rage and misery and protest that
> expressed itself in the thought; if I had not come it would have
> died like this: so why should I interfere. All over the bush things
> like this happen; they happen all the time; this is how life goes on,
> by living things dying in anguish. He gripped the gun between
> his knees and felt in his own limbs the myriad swarming pain of

the twitching animal that could no longer feel, and set his teeth,
and said over and over again under his breath: I can't stop it.
I can't stop it. There is nothing I can do.

Jim spoke for the first time in this session:

> '*He gripped the gun between his knees and felt in his own limbs the myriad
> swarming pain of the twitching animal that could no longer feel.*' He gets
> the pain while the buck can't. If you see something like that,
> you're taking on the pain and the feelings of that animal aren't
> you? You're taking them on – because [Jim presses his fist
> against his chest] you can *feel* the pain.

Jim is himself in clear physical discomfort as he speaks—shifting in his
chair, his eyes screwed up, his face wincing. 'It's sickening,' Jim contin-
ues, grimacing at the word as he repeats it: 'Sickening'. He went on,
after a little while, saying he too had seen death:

> I've smelt death as well. That's a horrible thing. It was in an
> abattoir. It was in Australia and part of what was on the whole
> a good time in my life. But that abattoir was horrific, it really
> was. I think what made it even worse - the thing that played on
> my mind was - the innocence of the animals. They were sheep
> and they were…standing there – but they weren't tied up or
> anything. They could walk around. And one by one, they had
> their throats slit, while the others were just - watching. And it's
> like they never processed it, the dumb animals, there was noth-
> ing they could do about it. And the fact that they weren't trying
> to escape or anything – That's what played on my mind, for a
> long, long time. The feller that was doing it, said to me, the
> more you do it, the better you get. It was nothing to him.

Jim's own pain condition began after he received surgery following an
injury. But its chronic nature, the pain's continuing years beyond the
healing of the initial physical trauma, is down to something sensitive
in him. Here, what he is sensitive to in turn, is the helplessness of the
animals, just as it pained him when the child, in the Bowen story,
could not stop the clock but had to wait for the mother's death.

The person leading the group points to the text. It was nothing to
the man used to killing the sheep, she says, and adds 'But in Lessing's

story, the boy says differently, "There is nothing I can do".' Jim replied that he knew that:

> But seeing the sheep in that abattoir, I don't think I've come to terms with that really, I haven't been able to reason with it, you see.

The memory seems to linger with him, maybe as his pain often does. But he says: 'That's a great story, it brought back some good, some bad things.' Literature deals in what cannot be reasoned with. Its tough use*less*ness in the face of experience—its power to hold together life's content without expectation of final coherence—is what makes it use*ful* for those who know they must live without answers or resolutions.

The group leader later looked at the recording of Jim's response, and was struck especially by the tone, she said, of his remark 'It's like they never processed it, the dumb animals'. She remembered what it reminded her of. A formal literary version of the experience Jim recounts goes like this—Gavin Ewart's poem, 'The Dying Animals':

> The animals that look at us like children
> In innocence, in perfect innocence!
> The innocence that looks at us! Like children
> the animals, the simple animals,
> have no idea why legs no longer work.
>
> The food that is refused, the love of sleeping –
> in innocence, in childhood innocence
> there is a parallel of love. Of sleeping
> they're never tired, the dying animals,
> sick children too, whose play to them is work.
>
> The animals are little children dying,
> brash tigers, household pets – all innocence,
> the flames that lit their eyes are also dying,
> the animals, the simple animals, -
> die easily; but hard for us, like work!

This verse is not 'free' but an adaptation of a medieval-Elizabethan lyric form, the sestina, which uses an intricate pattern of repeated words and phrases. The internal repetition of the words which end lines 1 and 3 is duplicated in all three stanzas—'children...children', 'sleeping...sleeping', 'dying...dying'; and there is repetition across the stanzas of the words which end lines 2, 4, and 5, 'innocence', 'animals', 'work'. This craft is how a poet makes meaningful *work* out of something, the bare elements of life at the level of simple event. The animals *'have no idea'*; like Jim, 'can't reason with' the experience. The poet can, though it is 'hard for us'.

'The reality of things – be thankful – only visits us for a brief while', says Graham Swift's protagonist in *Waterland*.[5] Too much reality may kill us; too little, and we are hardly alive. Poetry and fiction offer a middle place in which reality can visit, briefly and safely, but still as something consciously harder than usual, not as something easy or sanitized. 'The simple animals, -/die easily; but hard for us, like work!' So the verse form, though fluid, is itself hard, firm, 'a momentary stay against confusion,' as Robert Frost said of poetry.[6] But the animals, the children, the innocence, still move around, all versions of the same parallels. As the reader sees and hears these shifts, what he or she is almost inevitably reminded of is something *not* to do with childhood, animals or innocence: the tough work for adults. As in Jim, the knowledge is in adults, in lieu of children and animals. What hurts is the helplessness of being a mere witness to suffering, like the doctor who cannot cure. But the verse holds this together.

There is widespread rhetoric, running through philosophy and psychology, as well as literary studies and medical humanities, around readers' 'empathy' with literary texts. Empathy is defined by psychology as 'the experience of understanding another person's condition from their perspective', placing yourself in others' shoes and 'feeling what they are feeling'. Emotional identification with character and situation is prized for extending reflective powers and awareness of self and others and for improving 'helping behaviours'. Cognitive psychologists often relate engaged fiction-reading to the concept of 'Theory of Mind'—our ability to explain people's behaviour in terms of their thoughts, feelings, beliefs and desires. Fiction, suggests Lisa Zunshine, helps us better to navigate our social world by offering simulated opportunities for the exercise of Theory of Mind, a kind of 'cognitive workout', bestowing 'new knowledge and understanding of others' and a 'sharpened ethical sense'.[7]

But what happens inside the imaginative immersion of the readers we have witnessed is demonstrably much quicker and far less consciously voluntary than the vicarious 'sharing' of a fictional character's emotions. Mike, unable to stay in the room when he first heard John Clare's 'I Am'; Lois, thinking of the life she will never have while reading Robert Frost's 'The Road Not Taken'; Anthony, in relation to the David Constantine story, 'In Another Country', feeling residual grief for a past loss which he has long 'got over' at the level of ordinary functioning life. Reading the book *outside*, happens at the same moment, so to speak, as its reading the person *inside*. So, with the earliest literature, one examines the word in order to examine oneself. 'God hath spoken *once*; *twice* have I heard this' (Psalm 62:11).

A close analogy for this two-in-one process is when Jim's response to the short story suddenly triggered the thought of the poem, 'The Dying Animals' in the group leader. So it is that as a poem or a story goes on, at a specific instant something latent inside, at the back of the mind—it could be a thought, a memory, or another work of literature—is suddenly activated and aligned with it, silently, implicitly. There is no time for reflection. There is strictly speaking no thought, or no clear and complete one. What happens instead is an almost impossible, vertiginous simultaneity. The reader is still *the reader*—audience and witness to the text, which exists *outside*; but at the same time, the mind is the realizer of its own sudden inner message. When de Quincey heard the lines of Wordsworth—'carried far into his heart'—he said he felt that word 'far' suddenly opened up a whole inner world within him too.[8]

Read-aloud groups help show how vital this process of triggered echo is. Here, in a return to a favourite text and one moment of awakening in it, is what Heather said after she had read from the second movement of *A Christmas Carol*, when the Ghost of Christmas Past returns Scrooge to his childhood school room:

> It opened before them, and disclosed a long, bare, melancholy room, made barer still by lines of plain deal forms and desks. At one of these a lonely boy was reading near a feeble fire; and Scrooge sat down upon a form, and wept to see his poor forgotten self, as he used to be. 'Poor boy,' he said, and cried again.

The transcript of Heather's immediate response reads:

> He weeps for the boy's loneliness when, before, he couldn't feel
> his own. The boy is forgotten by others; but the man has forgot-
> ten *himself* - he's what's not there.

This is Scrooge seeing himself as innocent child, whilst being himself
hard adult: the two-in-one, the reader of himself affected by the
young boy in a way that softens and reanimates the older man. What
Heather is doing here is not merely making thematic or obvious links;
rather she is hearing the story's own second voice, the deep structure,
within its linear movements. At CRILS, we have become interested by
this process of reading the text and feeling a message within it. My
colleague, Philip Davis writes of it:

> Literature's language-within-language is formal and sophisti-
> cated. But what it triggers in the reader is almost its asymmet-
> rical opposite: a colloquial inner voice, a *second language* that is
> informally more crude, more like the immediate physical emo-
> tion of a shorthand, a coded message electrifyingly de-coded.[9]

This is why so often when reading, it is as if that deep second voice of
the text is inside *oneself.* Heather is a sufferer from depression: as with
Scrooge before the sight of his younger self, this text has a private
meaning for her. What the text locates at such moments is a species of
the 'inner voice' which novelist Marilynne Robinson seeks from the
members of her Iowa Writer's Workshop: 'the voice,' she says, 'without which one cannot be a writer'.

It is a clue that this special form of inner thinking is never finished.
Rather, it is what Eugene Gendlin calls thinking 'freshly at the edge of
the implicit'– not an exhausting of realizable things but a moment of
fleeting illumination, of remembering what is otherwise forgotten or
missed. Experiencing, says Gendlin, is always '*more than*' the categories
and the common phrases available for expression of it. So 'When no
concept seems to work, what more do you find?'

> Not disorder, not limbo, not some concept together with the
> opposite of that concept. Rather you find an intricacy, preg-
> nant, implicitly ordered, perhaps partly opaque.

When we try to speak from the intricacy, Gendlin says, we often
feel the strain of the implicit material coming through, and we have

trouble finding words. The words which do finally come are always more 'precise' than any default language. But still, the implicit is never merely defined and exhausted:

> The implicit never turns into something explicit as if it is now no longer there. Instead the words bring the implicit along with it, carry it forward. It is an always unfinished order that has to be taken along as we think.[10]

This 'thinking with the more', as Gendlin puts it—the inhabiting of matter that cannot ever be put safely under wraps—is what the readers we have witnessed quietly achieve. Their thought is not conclusive, offering definitive self-knowledge which can be contentedly possessed like self-help goals of realization; this is stored personal thinking that waits and needs to be touched off, realized again and again in live effect.

See, for a last example, what happened when Angela, a single mother in her twenties, was reading Elizabeth Gaskell's nineteenth-century novel, *Wives and Daughters*, a work as loyal as any I know to what must usually remain implicit and unspoken.

Squire Hamley has recently lost his wife, and his first-born and favoured son, Osborne, has come home to Hamley Hall having failed in his examinations at Cambridge. The Squire's underrated younger son, Roger, has also returned from Cambridge and, following a tense and unhappy family meal, Roger goes to his father's study and asks to share a pipe with him:

> The Squire sate and gazed into the embers, still holding his useless pipe stem. At last he said, in a low voice, as if scarcely aware he had got a visitor, - I used to write to her when she was away in London, and tell her the home news. But no letter will reach her now! Nothing reaches her!'
>
> Roger started up.
>
> 'Where's the tobacco box, father? Let me fill you another pipe!' and when he had done so, he stooped over his father and stroked his cheek. The squire shook his head.
>
> 'You've only just come home, lad,' the Squire says. 'You don't know me as I am nowadays! Any of the servants will tell you I'm not like the same man for getting into passions with them. I used to be reckoned a good master but that is past now! Osborne was

once a little boy, and she was once alive – and I was once a good master – a good master – yes! It is all past now.'

He took up his pipe, and began to smoke afresh, and Roger, after a silence of some minutes, began a long story about some Cambridge man's misadventure on the hunting-field, telling it with such humour that the Squire was beguiled into hearty laughing. When they rose to go to bed, his father said to Roger, -

'Well, we've had a pleasant evening – at least, I have. But perhaps you have not; for I'm but poor company now, I know.'

'I don't know when I've passed a happier evening, father,' said Roger. And he spoke truly, though he did not trouble himself to find out the cause of his happiness. (Chapter Twenty-three)

Angela noticed how Roger at first uses the male tradition of smoking a pipe together to help the Squire to relax, to bring him back to his usual self. The prose quietly intimates that this is the son's gently persevering way—he who at first feels to the Squire to be merely a 'visitor'—of trying to repair his father's feelings of 'useless' redundancy and loneliness. But then Roger finds the familiar ritual helping both of them, by allowing that tiny intimacy—'he stooped over his father and stroked his cheek'. It is a female touch, as though Roger were instinctively fulfilling the dead wife's ritual now.

'Roger is feeling better, too – more at home,' Angela said. 'After a while, they're both forgetting Osborne without meaning to. And that's – good. If they noticed, they wouldn't be so happy.' It's a recognition that the new intimacy of father and son is happening as quietly as it would in life, an undertone. Angela could see that Roger is 'starting to replace Osborne'—and even partly Mrs Hamley—simply by helping things to carry on as they have always done. This is good reading. Angela is intuitively appreciating the inexplicit family language which Tolstoy, as much as Gaskell, especially relished and which he called a 'special capacity'—a particularly subtle kind of 'mutual understanding'.[11] What makes this moment between Roger and the Squire wonderfully Tolstoyan is that Gaskell's apparently mundane human material half-reveals its really real content as a kind of sudden surprise. Yet that lovely surprise depends upon the reader's own capacity for mutual understanding. That's why something much more demanding is happening in Angela's response than readerly 'empathy'. Rather,

Angela is inhabiting the novel's undramatic family space almost as deftly as the author is doing.

Noticing this, the group leader points out how this understated event is made even more moving for resonating with a tiny under-event from much earlier in the novel and from the family's far past:

> When Roger caressed his mother, she used laughingly to allude
> to the fable of the lap-dog and the donkey; so thereafter he left
> off all demonstration of affection. (Chapter Four)

In Aesop's fable, a donkey covets the attention given to his master's petted dog, but, when he clumsily paws his master in hope of the same affection, he is beaten. The mother's mention of this fable to Roger was not really meant as a rebuff, for all the child's sense of rejection. 'It's as though,' said Angela, 'the love he once tried to give to his mother as a child has found its right place – going out to the father who feels her loss. And yet Roger won't know where that touch has come from, just as he doesn't know the cause of his happiness. It's like a deep, hidden family secret – a good one.' This moment of quiet fulfillment does indeed depend on so much that has happened secretly and silently over family time, within the novel's own deep memory. It is one way in which this book closely imitates life, holding its own stored emotional matter just under the surface narrative until it is ready to be remembered by story and reader, and not necessarily consciously by the protagonists themselves.

None of these people we have seen carefully reading has a degree in English; they're not affluent or thriving. At such moments, it seems almost an advantage that they do not have the resources of conventional education. In *Untimely Meditations*, Nietzsche says of the complacently cultured:

> He invents for his habits, modes of thinking, likes and dislikes,
> the general formula 'healthiness', and dismisses every uncom-
> fortable disturber of the peace as being sick and neurotic... On
> those occasions when he is honest with himself, even the philis-
> tine is aware that the philosophies his kind produce and bring to
> market are in many ways spiritless, though they are of course
> extremely healthy and profitable.[12]

The fact that these readers have not profited much in the conventional ways has no doubt added to their difficulties. But it does mean that, by contrast with the habitual modes of thinking of the semi-cultured, these are people whose intelligence is triggered exceptionally by the literary stimulus in ways that could not be predicted, even or especially by themselves.

But struggle is not everything; there is happiness in this. Angela has a long history of mental illness, and her chief anxiety is that her son, Luis, has only ever seen her as someone who is helpless or incapable. When, as part of the research study involving this group, Angela saw a video-recording of this moment, the interviewer pointed out how happy Angela herself looked when saying 'That's good'. 'I wish Luis could see me just as I look there,' she said. We don't know if she was thinking of Roger as a sort of Luis.

These are themselves 'good' moments, we researchers find: when a person not only shows what they are capable of but also sees it for himself or herself in the video clips. These interviews, we've come to conclude, have a therapeutic value of their own. They do not cure, any more than the literature does; rather, in re-creating the instant of reading, they help to release or access once again the vital capacity first stimulated by the poem or book. These moments are too individual, too alive and too emotionally earned to go by the name of comfortable 'healthy-mindedness' or the utilitarian prescriptions of 'positive thinking'. 'Outcomes' are not the point here. It does not matter, at one level, that Angela's wish that her child could see her 'just as I look there' can't be practically fulfilled. The thought of it alone is a good.

But something did come of this. Angela's son found this Wordsworth fragment. It had been read in the same session as the chapter from *Wives and Daughters* and Angela had taken it home with her:

> My heart leaps up when I behold
>   A rainbow in the sky:
> So was it when my life began;
> So is it now I am a man;
> So be it when I shall grow old,
>   Or let me die!

'He picked it up and started to read it out loud, the way children always like to read,' Angela recalled at interview:

And I could see it, the instant his eye moved from the end of the first line to the second. It was as if the word was just waiting there to surprise him. 'I behold – a *rainbow*'. The excitement burst out from his voice and he smiled and looked up at me, and I smiled too.

Both mother and son here know something deep about the importance of lineation in verse. The moment passes but its effects do not. It is as Deleuze said of Spinoza and the passions:

> You are affected with joy. Your power of acting is increased. The affects of joy are like a springboard, they make us pass through something that we would never have been able to pass if there had only been sadnesses. In this sense joy makes one intelligent.[13]

Joy's springboard—that is also one of the most important and vital uses for poetry in the world, as an instinct for life.

****

Reading, says Mark Edmundson is 'life's grand second chance' for people whose first start has not given them what they need.[14] The advent of that possible second go at life—sometimes the merest hint or spark of it—is one of the most inspiriting things about the examples of powerful reading I have considered in this book.

But what troubles me most is that, for every one of these unaccustomed readers, there are countless others—non-readers—who often have no such chance. It is more usual to have no trigger or help in the face of the inarticulately real, whether it be from a book or a person. It is far more common for people to have to bear and suffer alone, unsupported by an external language and witness. The novelists and poets know this. There is a doctor in George Eliot's *Middlemarch*, who has to hear Dorothea ask him, when she knows her husband is dying, to tell her what she can do. It is a 'cry from soul to soul', in what is otherwise a 'troublous fitfully illuminated life'. 'But what could he say?' is Lydgate's inward response (Chapter 30). I have been arguing that the capacity of the realist novel simply to repeat this experience, helps it.

It can seem an odd thing for adults to do—reading fiction for the sake of some good. Even Tolstoy thought so at times. 'It's funny that I should even think about writing a story at all,' Tolstoy said in midlife, when he had taken over the family estate: 'I waste my adult years writing stories when I can and must and want to get down to business.' Why on earth would a grown-up spend so much time on something as apparently 'soft' as fiction? But when he was doing it rather than thinking about it, he more often found that writing *was* the business, 'the best activity in the world', because involuntarily, it was the thing he could not *live* without. Literature then was not child's play: 'One ought only to write when one leaves a piece of one's own flesh in the inkpot, each time one dips one's pen.'[15]

What occurs to me now is that the read-aloud groups I have been describing, help to create in a little community the kind of readers that George Eliot and Tolstoy wrote for and sought alone—readers whose first concern is the serious business of living, not the mere consumption of books as an end or an escape or a pastime in itself. The groups help to realize and solidify the virtual communities of separated readers which George Eliot envisaged. 'The only effect I ardently long to produce by my writings,' she wrote, 'is that those who read them should be able to *feel* the pains of those who differ from themselves in everything but the *broad* fact of being struggling, erring creatures.'[16] They re-create the space within the world that the book tries to create in the individual—where meaning is handed on and translated personally.

****

But these groups do not just happen by chance in the world. They themselves need to be created if reading is to be encouraged against the odds. It is not that one cannot understand people's resistance, fear or disdain; helped by a poem indeed!

If the work I have been describing is to be carried on, something practical needs to be put in place for the future. The starting point for such practical implementation is in part the teaching of literature in universities.

There needs to be more space on the English curriculum for *doing* reading, seriously and deeply. This is *work*, a craft, almost as demanding as writing itself, and—when readers are inhabiting the difficult emotional terrain out of which serious writing comes—analogous to it. The intent readers we have witnessed in their reading-groups who are experiencing varying degrees of physical and psychological trauma, give extra force to Ted Hughes' famous description of poetry as 'at bottom, in every recorded case, the voice of pain'. The sometimes raw inarticulacy of these readers is in imitation of the processes of writers themselves at core, where expression is a hard-won achievement—the struggling means, as Hughes put it, 'by which the poet tries to reconcile that pain with the world'.[17]

You would think this core experience—though surely not always pain—would be the first thing on a university course. It isn't: most students are expected to have introductory courses on 'theory'. The literary text has become increasingly incidental to the pushing of prior agendas and approaches that reduce naivety; one colleague told me she 'rarely opens the book when teaching'. Instead, attentive reading is dismissed as old-fashioned 'close reading', and serious reading is everywhere professionalized. It is 'impossible', another colleague assured me, to read *Paradise Lost* without scholarly notes.

There is less and less evidence of university English teachers being what Mark Edmundson, himself an English Literature professor, insists they can be, in *Why Read?*—namely, the best advocate for a book in class. 'The objective of interpretation is to bring the past into the present and to do so in a way that will make the writer's ghost nod in something like approval. This means operating with the author's terms, thinking, insofar as it is possible, the writer's thoughts, reclaiming his world through his language'. The good teacher's 'inspired ventriloquism', Edmundson suggests, is like Sassall's achievement in relation to his patients: he 'becomes' or impersonates the author for the sake of bringing the past vision alive into the present for transmission and use.[18]

One of the disconcerting surprises of my own teaching life is that it is the medical students I teach who expect to be emotionally moved and challenged by the literature we read together: that's why they opt for these courses—'to feel something human again', as they put it, amid a surfeit of learned abstractions about human life. When I teach undergraduate literature students, on the other hand, they expect historical context, literary theory, or second-order 'themes': they have been trained to eschew feeling. Get them off-message, however, and they'll tell you the reason they chose English was because of a book they 'love'.

I don't want to educate readers out of that love: I want to make of it, instead, a discipline; to put feeling to *use* in the way we have seen relatively novice readers use immediate and often involuntary personal responses—as the starting place for hard and serious thinking. The teaching of university English generally misses out that first crucial thing—the powerful emotional place inside the reader which, summoned by the literary work, is in imitation and memory of the emotional source out of which the writing itself first comes. English Literature departments, of all things, should not be, as they sometimes can be, the places where literature has become most alienated from its human origins—where formal thinking substitutes for deep nonformal thinking inside a literary work. The quest for today's originality in literary studies—the new ideological take or template through which to 'interrogate' texts—is too often tomorrow's dead end. The truly original thinking is that which recovers the human-emotional *origin* of literary works through sudden vital recognitions. It is just that the thinking should start from the right place.

But what I am urging here is not confined to secondary and tertiary educational pedagogy: it comprises a public service and a human duty. The emotional space for serious thinking which literary writing and reading constitutes, is missing not from literature departments only, but, generally speaking, from too much of the world. Many of us do not have a place or a mode called 'Serious' to which we can readily turn when we might need it, and certainly not one that stays as close to the realities of experienced life as does poetry or fiction. I am speaking for myself here: literature and literary reading are possibly the best forms of thinking that humans in need or trouble will ever have. They are more *special* than special*ist*. Literary works themselves are special, in the sense that the language is not normal but *un*usual and often testing in the light of the special occasion of literature and the experience that prompts it. Such books thus written stop their subject matter from being taken for granted or dismissed as merely ordinary or unprized. But a reader's own deepest sense is special too, and often not ordinarily available or accessible in the sudden ways a poem or story can activate.

The special thing literature can do in the world desperately needs representation, active encouragement, a model of involvement, and the tradition of English in universities is uniquely placed to offer such help. Indeed, if university English became more specialized in the good way I have described—in learning reading as a concentrated craft—it could become less specialized in every other way. This practical speciality of attention, as I have tried to show through my examples of non-specialized readers, really can be taken back out into the world where literature belongs and has its subjects and its origins.

Some English students I am teaching do exactly that: as part of their course, they practise shared reading outside the university—in community libraries, residential care homes, schools, and recovery units—with people who would not normally read at all or do not know how to read. The purpose is not to spread 'culture' in some condescending imperialist manner for those supposed to be in need even when they hardly recognize it. The work of these volunteers is more modestly artisan—to spread, informally, the craft of excited reading and see if it catches people. This is crucial. The modern habit of quick scanning, of 'light' reading, leaves voices and thoughts silenced. Careful and caring reading, by contrast, across the range and depth of literary material, energizes what is otherwise kept enfolded within books and latent inside people.

Some of these students now have careers as readers. The Reader Organization employs literature graduates as readers in residence. They offer weekly shared reading to residents in care homes, to service-users in mental health hospitals and health centres, to men and women in prison, to looked-after children; and they provide training to professionals within those areas to have the confidence to use a seventeenth-century poem in a twenty-first century setting.

In summary: I do want a widening remit for literature; I don't want it to be a merely academic specialism; I do want it to go out into the world. But I don't want it *not* to be a special, careful act of attention that uses feeling to get to deeper thought.

Equivalently, I also want to recap upon two key dangers that arise from making literature useful: one occurs within universities, and the other out in the world.

In medical humanities as an academic discipline, literature is regarded as a resource from which trainee doctors can either glean professionally relevant knowledge—insight into particular conditions, models for humane doctoring, understanding of how diverse cultures deal with disease and death—and/or learn specific skills, such as 'clinical empathy', critical reflection, improved communication skills. The chief problem here, I have argued, is the using of fiction and poetry for predetermined ends. Students are encouraged to scan or raid books for their thematic or transferable content. They are neither required nor expected to read books carefully as a personally immersed and committed experience without clear goals or lessons immediately in sight. Real reading, as we have seen, does not know its own aims or purposes in advance; it has no idea of explicit end-points. Rather thoughts and meanings formulate themselves, emergently arising *out of* the reading process—useful but not instrumental, resonant but not pious or didactic.

Secondly, there are hazards in the spread of serious reading beyond universities when it is packaged as a cure and called 'bibliotherapy'. Directing people to read particular books for specific problems, helpful though such guidance might at first appear to people who are not accustomed to reading, is not actually serving people in trouble. One of the gifts of a poem or story is that it is entirely neutral so far as the reader is concerned; a poem neither knows nor cares whether the person is well or ill, and has no plan or programme to accomplish in respect to its reader. Any therapeutic effect of literature arises precisely from literature's never trying or meaning to be a therapy. The kind of revivifying help for self which literature across the full range of genres and ages can provide—in place of targeted self-help books and as an adjunct or alternative to doctors, counsellors, therapists—is never exclusive to 'ill' people, nor aimed at cure or specific relevance.

Health here is not just healthy-mindedness; any more than literature is just about problems or sorrows. Health is not just about cures for illnesses. It is about letting in and giving out more life and more thought, and finding space and a place in which to think everything and anything.

Notes

1. John Berger, *A Fortunate Man* (London: Granta Books, 1967), pp. 158–9.
2. John Berger, *The Guardian*, 13 Dec 2013, p. 17.
3. Reprint with Afterword published by Royal College of Practitioners, 2003.
4. Marcel Proust, *On Reading*, trans. and ed. by Jean Autret and William Burford (New York: The Macmillan Company, 1971), p. 35.
5. Graham Swift, *Waterland* (London: Picador, 1992), p. 33.

6. From 'The Figure a Poem Makes', 1939, in *The Collected Prose of Robert Frost*, ed. by Mark Richardson (Cambridge, Mass.: Harvard University Press, 2007), p. 132.

7. Lisa Zunshine, *Why We Read Fiction: Theory of Mind and the Novel* (Columbus: Ohio State University Press, 2006), pp. 159–64.

8. Thomas De Quincey, *Recollections of Lakes and Lake Poets*, 1834–40, edited by David Wright (Harmondsworth: Middlesex: Penguin Books Ltd, 1972) p. 161.

9. Philip Davis, *Reading and the Reader* (Oxford: Oxford University Press, 2014), p. 35.

10. Eugene Gendlin, 'The New Phenomenology of Carrying Forward', *Continental Philosophy Review*, 37:1, 127–51, pp. 127–30, 134–5.

11. Leo Tolstoy, *Childhood, Boyhood, Youth* (1857), trans. Rosemary Edmonds (Harmondsworth, Middlesex: Penguin Books, Ltd, 1964), p. 263.

12. Friedrich Nietzsche, *Untimely Meditations,* trans. R. J. Hollingdale (Cambridge; Cambridge University Press, 1983), p. 12.

13. *The Lectures of Gilles Deleuze*. 'On Spinoza' (1978). Available at: http://deleuzelectures.blogspot.co.uk/2007/02/on-spinoza.html.

14. Mark Edmundson, 'The Risk of Reading' *New York Times*, 1 August 2004.

15. *Tolstoy's Letters*, edited by R. F. Christian, 2 vols (New York: Charles Scribner's Sons), vol. 1, p. 129, 133; Henri Troyat, *Tolstoy*, trans. by Nancy Amphoux (Harmondsworth: Penguin Books Ltd, 1967), p. 394.

16. *The George Eliot Letters*, edited by G. S. Haight, 9 vols (New Haven: Yale University Press, 1954–78), vol. iii, p. 111.

17. *The Letters of Ted Hughes*, selected and edited by Christopher Reid (London: Faber and Faber, 2009), p. 458.

18. Mark Edmundson, *Why Read?* (New York: Bloomsbury, 2004), p. 53.

Acknowledgements

I wish to thank The Reader and its recipients for making possible the writing of some of this book.

Copyright Acknowledgements

From The Poetry of Robert Frost, edited by Edward Connery Lathem. Reproduced by permission of The Random House Group Ltd.

Excerpts from 'The Road Not Taken' from the book THE POETRY OF ROBERT FROST edited by Edward Connery Lathem. Copyright © 1916, 1969 by Henry Holt and Company, copyright © 1944 by Robert Frost. Reprinted by permission of Henry Holt and Company, LLC. All rights reserved.

For 'The Dying Animals' – From Gavin Ewart, Collected Poems 1980–90, by permission of the estate of Gavin Ewart.

For extract from 'In Another Country' – From David Constantine *Under the Dam and Other Stories*, Comma Press, 2005.

Select Bibliography

The literary works which matter for this book will be apparent throughout. I list here the works which have most influenced my thinking around them.

Balint, Michael, *The Doctor, His Patient and the Illness* (London: Pitman Publishing Ltd, 1957).

Berger, J., *A Fortunate Man*, 1967 (Cambridge: Granta Books, 1989).

Bergson, Henri, *Creative Evolution*, 1911 (New York: Dover Publications Inc, 1998).

Bion, Wilfred R., *Experiences in Groups*, 1961 (London: Routledge, 1994).

Bion, Wilfred R., *Learning from Experience* (London: Maresfield Library, 1962).

Bion, Wilfred R., *Transformations: Change from Learning to Growth* (London: Heinemann, 1965).

Bion, Wilfred R., *Second Thoughts* (London: Maresfield Library, 1967).

Bion, Wilfred R., *Attention and Interpretation* (London: Maresfield Library, 1970).

Burton, Robert, *The Anatomy of Melancholy*, ed. Thomas C. Faulkner, Nicolas K. Kiessling and Rhonda L. Blair (Oxford: Clarendon Press, 1989).

Heidegger, Martin, *Being and Time*, 1953 (New York: SUNY Press).

James, William, *The Varieties of Religious Experience*, 1902 (Harmondsworth, Middlesex: Penguin Books Ltd, 1985).

Kierkegaard, Søren, *The Sickness Unto Death*, 1849, trans. Alastair Hannay (Harmondsworth, Middlesex: Penguin Books Ltd, 1989).

Nagel, Thomas, *The View from Nowhere* (Oxford: Oxford University Press, 1986).

Spinoza, Benedictus de, *Ethics*, 1677, trans. George Eliot (Salzburg: University of Salzburg, 1981).

Tolstoy, Leo, *What is Art?*, 1898, trans. Richard Pevear (Harmondsworth, Middlesex: Penguin Books Ltd, 1995).

Index